STRONG FOUNDATIONS IN EARLY MATHEMATICS

Sara Miller McCune founded SAGE Publishing in 1965 to support the dissemination of usable knowledge and educate a global community. SAGE publishes more than 1000 journals and over 800 new books each year, spanning a wide range of subject areas. Our growing selection of library products includes archives, data, case studies and video. SAGE remains majority owned by our founder and after her lifetime will become owned by a charitable trust that secures the company's continued independence.

Los Angeles | London | New Delhi | Singapore | Washington DC | Melbourne

STRONG FOUNDATIONS IN EARLY MATHEMATICS

LORNA EARLE
SAM PARKES

Learning Matters
A SAGE Publishing Company
1 Oliver's Yard
55 City Road
London EC1Y 1SP

SAGE Publications Inc.
2455 Teller Road
Thousand Oaks, California 91320

SAGE Publications India Pvt Ltd
B 1/I 1 Mohan Cooperative Industrial Area
Mathura Road
New Delhi 110 044

SAGE Publications Asia-Pacific Pte Ltd
3 Church Street
#10-04 Samsung Hub
Singapore 049483

First published in 2023

Library of Congress Control Number: 2022945334

British Library Cataloguing in Publication Data

A catalogue record for this book is available from the British Library

Editor: Amy Thornton
Senior project editor: Chris Marke
Project management: TNQ Technologies
Marketing manager: Lorna Patkai
Cover design: Victoria Bridal
Typeset by: TNQ Technologies
Printed in the UK

ISBN: 978-1-5297-9120-4
ISBN: 978-1-5297-9119-8 (pbk)

CONTENTS

CONTENTS MAP

Whilst the chapters are organised sequentially, this map shows how they connect together to support the development of a rounded subject knowledge for the teaching of mathematics.

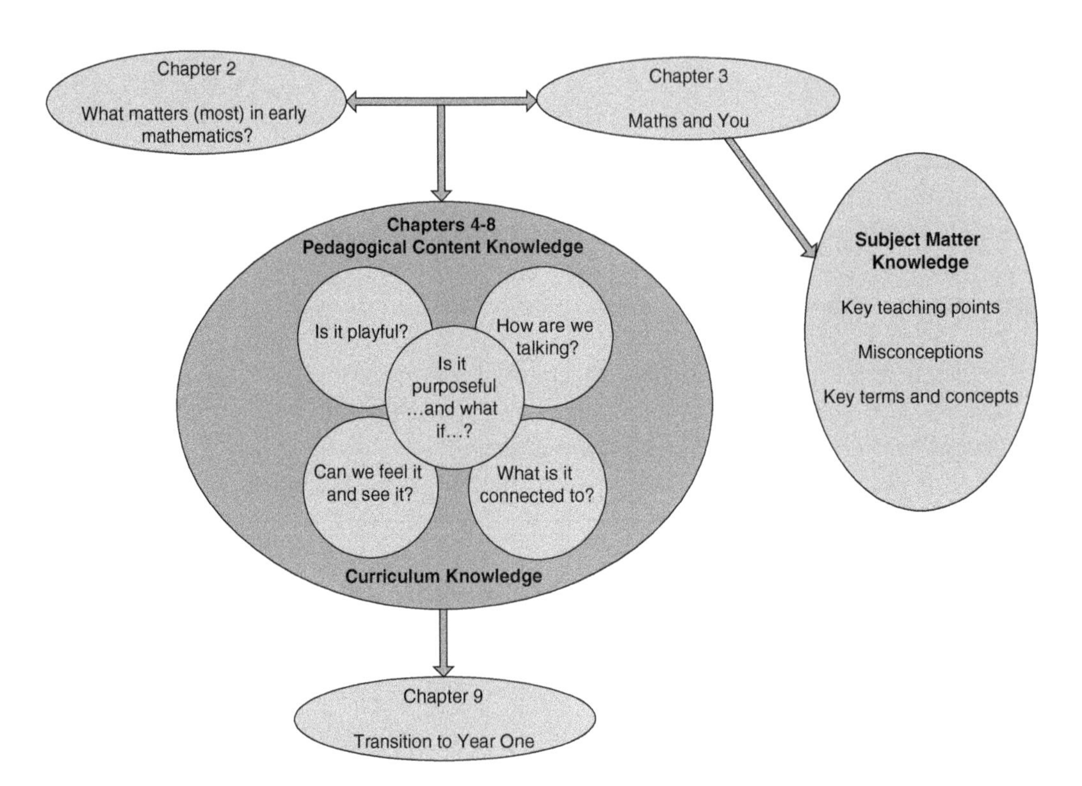

ACKNOWLEDGEMENTS

We acknowledge with gratitude the contributions to the creation of this book of many specialist organisations, colleagues, school partners, trainees, friends and children (including our own, to whom we dedicate this work). You have generously shared your experiences, viewpoints, questions and time and we hope we have done this justice. With particular thanks to the teachers and children of Reception classes across the University of Chichester Academy Trust – thank you for letting us come and play!

FOREWORD

I was delighted to be asked to write the foreword for such a significant book. I have worked in Early Years for over 35 years, and my career has included teaching on childcare and Early Years teaching programmes in both further education and later higher education institutions. Over this time, I have seen first-hand a lack of mathematical confidence in many students and Early Years educators, and these feelings mirrored my own for many years until I finally confronted the challenge and gained a mathematics GCSE way after leaving school. This qualification positively impacted not only my career but also my ability to feel that I could legitimately and effectively promote the teaching of mathematics within the Early Years and beyond.

The book intentionally focuses on the Reception year, a period recognised by Ofsted (2018) as fundamental to children's success, and as such provides a key text for aspiring and employed Reception educators. Texts written specifically for this unique year group are surprisingly rare and, for a complex year group, absolutely vital. The Reception year often lacks a sense of belonging, standing apart from preschool while, quite rightly, being part of the Early Years Foundation Stage (EYFS) and yet also separated from the rest of the school by the discontinuity of pedagogy created by the change of framework from EYFS to National Curriculum (Nicholson, 2019). Despite this focus, the book has much to offer educators working within the preschool sector and those in Key Stage 1. It offers insight, clarity and good practice ideas along with suggested professional learning activities and reflections throughout. The principles and practices are sound for the teaching of mathematics across age groups and phases. The chapters offer the educator the opportunity to gain a broader view of mathematics that in turn could enable them to identify and confidently act on teachable moments that engage young children's mathematical thinking.

This book supports Early Years teachers and practitioners to build strong foundations in mathematics for themselves and the children they teach. It focuses on the development of teacher subject knowledge as a keystone for enhancing children's learning and development in mathematics. The book supports trainee teachers, Early Years students and practising teachers to reflect on their own mathematics learning and consider how this influences their teaching and subject confidence. It explores subject-specific pedagogies and how these can be most effectively synthesised with the uniqueness of Early Years practice holding the pedagogy of play as central to effective teaching and learning. Importantly, the book celebrates the innate mathematician in every human, at every stage of their learning.

Debra Laxton, Senior Lecturer in Education -
Early Childhood Lead, University of Chichester.

ABOUT THE AUTHORS

LORNA EARLE Lorna is a qualified teacher for both primary and secondary age ranges, who has always specialised in mathematics. Lorna began her teaching career in primary school where she was the mathematics lead, responsible for developing curriculum provision for all age groups. Lorna is currently a Senior Lecturer in Primary Education specialising and leading in mathematics at the University of Chichester. She teaches on both undergraduate and postgraduate ITE courses. Lorna's research interests include focusing on the importance of developing conceptual understanding to support formal methods in mathematics and the effective teaching and learning of times tables.

SAM PARKES Sam became a primary mathematics subject leader during her fourth year of teaching, despite a historically negative relationship with the subject, and has gradually grown to enjoy and champion the teaching of mathematics since that point. She is currently a Senior Lecturer and Primary Maths Specialist working as part of the ITE department at the University of Chichester. Sam teaches on the primary undergraduate and postgraduate programmes and works with a wide range of schools to support improvements in mathematics with both the University's Academy Trust and local school partners. Her research interests include collaborative professional development, leading and managing sustainable change and developing inclusive community cultures, advocating for the empowerment and agency of teachers across the profession.

INTRODUCTION

Teachers matter more than other factors, and teachers in the Early Years matter the most. So, teachers of early mathematics have to use the best pedagogical strategies...Every strategy, from play to direct instruction, can be educative or mis-educative.

(Clements & Sarama, 2018)

We have more than 30 years' experience between us of teaching mathematics to children, to trainee Early Years educators and primary teachers, and to qualified teachers and in supporting the leadership of and professional development in mathematics across dozens of schools. However, mindful of the following maxim pinned on our office wall (which of course is equally applicable to women!):

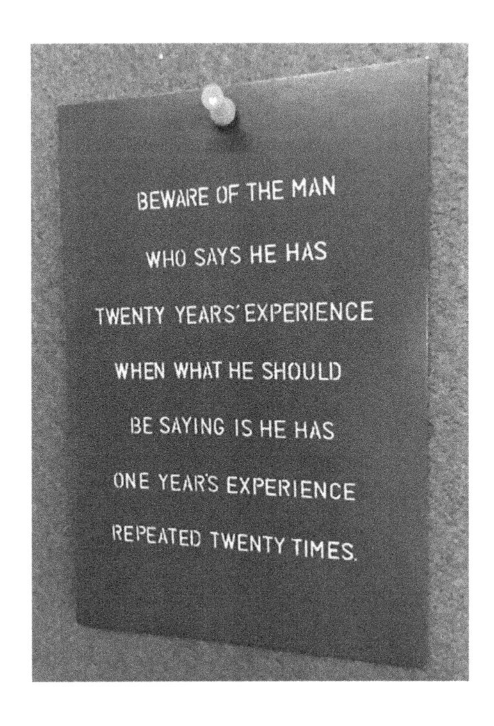

we are continually working to expand and strengthen our knowledge and expertise. This book is a result of our focused engagement on the teaching and learning of early mathematics. We have engaged with reams of research material, professional texts and sources, listened to Early Years colleagues and mathematics specialists, talked with our students and school partners and had the privilege of spending time with many children to observe and join in with their mathematical learning. In collating these, we hope to offer a useful summary of and guide to the best pedagogical strategies for mathematical development in the Early Years, with a particular focus on the Reception year.

The Reception year was our core focus for five reasons:

1. Recent changes to the Early Years Foundation Stage and Early Learning Goals
2. The growing attention being paid to the idea of a 'unique Reception year'
3. A culmination of experiences and knowledge of research evidence that suggests a prevalence of low mathematical confidence in trainees who choose to specialise in Early Years or lower primary age phases
4. An awareness that specific mathematical subject knowledge development for our Early Years specialists was lacking
5. A concern that a growing emphasis on 'number' and 'memory' could result in a narrowing oversimplification of the rich and complex world of 'mathematics'.

The work of the Early Childhood Maths Group (ECMG) and the 'Maths is More' working group strongly resonates with our thoughts and experiences, and we recommend their summaries of and response documents to issues related to these five points in the 'Further Reading' below.

We come to mathematics ourselves through fairly polar opposite routes; Lorna has always loved mathematics and has learned it herself to a high level, Sam's experiences and relationship with the subject was considerably less positive until becoming a maths leader of her primary school prompted enrolment onto the Primary Maths Specialist Teacher programme (MaST) in its first year – an experience that finally succeeded in re-lighting a fire for maths teaching and learning that was almost extinguished. As a result of our experiences, we share a determination to play our part in ensuring that all our students, the teachers we support in school and consequently the children that they care for every day are not limited in their mathematical lives by fear, shame or anxiety. We strive to include and empower everyone we have the opportunity to work with and welcome any chance to discuss and develop our collective understanding of mathematics teaching and learning. This book is our contribution to that continuing conversation.

ACTIVITY

Consider your view of the subject of mathematics. What objects/images/places... share features or elements that are similar to your view of maths?

You are creating a metaphor, your metaphor, for the subject.

Some examples we have heard over the years are below.

> *Maths is like a set of building blocks; you have to get the basics in place before you can build on them.*
>
> *I see it like a maze, lots of different pathways, some are dead ends, some are shortcuts, and I can get very lost!*
>
> *It's like a cliff face that I have to climb, and some of the ledges and footholds and plants I can grab to get to the top are more secure than others...*
>
> *I think maths is like a jigsaw puzzle. There are many different smaller pieces and they all fit together to make a bigger picture.*
>
> *Maths is like forest, lots of trees that build on strong roots upwards which co-exist and interconnect with other plants and animals in different ways.*
>
> *It's like a Jenga tower. You can build on different ideas, and they all depend on each other and even if some are missing it can still stand but if you take away too many pieces, or there are big gaps then it all crashes down.*
>
> *I see maths as a collection of ski runs, there are different routes to the bottom, and some are harder than others. I can choose which route I want to take but if someone makes me take a harder route than I'm ready for it could be scary.*
>
> *It's like the tube map for me...*
>
> *I think it's like the ocean, you can just dive in and swim in it. There are currents that can take you in different directions, and interesting and beautiful things to notice and explore along the way.*

FURTHER READING

ECMG. (2020). *Response to EYFSP consultation 2019/20.* https://earlymaths.org/response-to-eyfsp-consultation/

Maths is More Working Group. (2022). *Maths is more.* https://www.atm.org.uk/write/MediaUploads/ATM%20News/FINAL_Maths_is_More_24June2022_(1).pdf

REFERENCE

Clements, D., & Sarama, J. (2018). Myths of early math. *Education Sciences*, *8*(2), 71.

PART 1

MATHEMATICAL LANDSCAPES AND FOUNDATIONS

INTRODUCTION TO PART 1

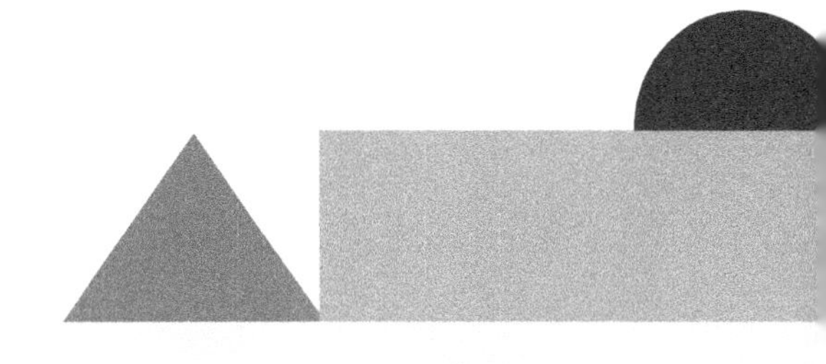

MATHEMATICAL LANDSCAPES AND FOUNDATIONS

In the first three chapters of this book, we will explore some of the big contextual and personal ideas that can be helpful to consider when strengthening your own foundations for teaching and learning mathematics.

'Chapter 1: The Current Landscape of Early Mathematics Education' gives an overview of the current context surrounding early mathematics and outlines key resources and materials that contribute to Early Years practice in mathematics.

'Chapter 2: What Matters (Most) in Early Mathematics?' supports you to consider the purpose of mathematics education, and how this influences early mathematical learning.

'Chapter 3: Maths and You' invites you to consider the importance of your relationship with mathematics, explore key ideas of mathematical subject matter knowledge, pedagogical content knowledge and curriculum knowledge and outlines key subject-matter knowledge for effective teaching and learning of mathematics in the Reception year.

1

THE CURRENT LANDSCAPE OF EARLY MATHEMATICS EDUCATION

CHAPTER OBJECTIVES

- Gain an overview of the current context surrounding early mathematics
- Outline key resources and materials that contribute to the mathematics education landscape for Early Years practice

INTRODUCTION

There have been far-reaching developments in the broader context surrounding mathematics teaching in the UK spanning the last decade; from the introduction of a revised National Curriculum, through the increasing dissemination and prevalence of a 'mastery' approach and nationwide 'maths hubs', to more recent changes in statutory policy documentation and guidance documents for mathematics in the Early Years.

EXPLORING STATUTORY DOCUMENTATION

Department
for Education

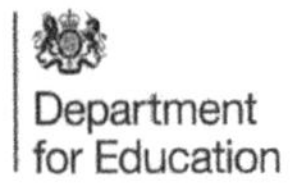

Statutory framework for the early years foundation stage

Setting the standards for learning, development and care for children from birth to five

Published: 31 March 2021

Effective: 1 September 2021

1

Figure 1.1

The Early Years Foundation Stage (EYFS) framework (DfE, 2021) is built on four guiding principles: the unique child, positive relationships, enabling environments, and learning and development. With specific regard to mathematical learning and development, it states that, *'Developing a strong grounding in number is essential so that all children develop the necessary building blocks to excel mathematically. Children should be able to count confidently, develop a deep understanding of the numbers to 10, the relationships between them and the patterns within those numbers. By providing frequent and varied opportunities to build and apply this understanding such as using manipulatives, including small pebbles and tens frames for organising counting children will develop a secure base of knowledge and vocabulary from which mastery of mathematics is built. In addition, it is important that the curriculum includes rich opportunities for children to develop their spatial reasoning skills across all areas of mathematics including shape, space and measures. It is important that children develop positive attitudes and interests in mathematics, look for patterns and relationships, spot connections, 'have a go', talk to adults and peers about what they notice and not be afraid to make mistakes.'*

It also outlines the expected level of development for children at the end of the EYFS in the form of Early Learning Goals (ELGs). In mathematics, outcomes in number and number patterns are listed:

ELG: Number

Children at the expected level of development will:

- Have a deep understanding of numbers up to 10, including the composition of each number;
- Subitise (recognise quantities without counting) up to 5;
- Automatically recall (without reference to rhymes, counting or other aids) number bonds up to 5 (including subtraction facts) and some number bonds to 10, including double facts.

ELG: Numerical Patterns

Children at the expected level of development will:

- Verbally count beyond 20, recognising the pattern of the counting system;
- Compare quantities up to 10 in different contexts, recognising when one quantity is greater than, less than or the same as the other quantity;
- Explore and represent patterns within numbers up to 10, including evens and odds, double facts and how quantities can be distributed equally (p. 13–14).

Since 2014, as a result of significant resource allocation to the NCETM (National Centre for Excellence in the Teaching of Mathematics), around 9,000 primary schools have adopted certain principles and pedagogical practices, under the term 'mastery', into their mathematics teaching. The NCETM define 'mastery' as follows:

> *Mastering maths means pupils of all ages acquiring a deep, long-term, secure and adaptable understanding of the subject. The phrase 'teaching for mastery' describes the elements of classroom practice and school organisation that combine to give pupils the best chances of mastering maths. Achieving mastery means acquiring a solid enough understanding of the maths that's been taught to enable pupils to move on to more advanced material.*
>
> (NCETM, 2022)

They outline '5 Big Ideas' that underpin and scaffold mathematics learning within a mastery approach,

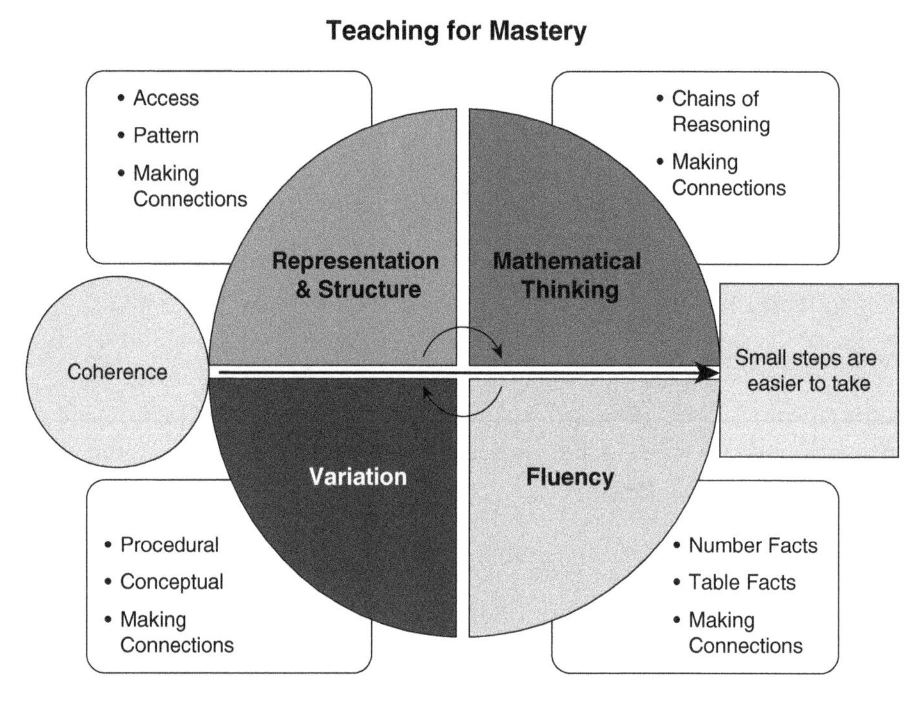

Figure 1.2

> *Coherence – Lessons are broken down into small, connected steps that gradually unfold the concept, providing access for all children and leading to a generalisation of the concept and the ability to apply the concept to a range of contexts.*
>
> *Representation and Structure – Representations used in lessons expose the mathematical structure being taught, the aim being that students can do the maths without recourse to the representation.*
>
> *Mathematical Thinking – If taught ideas are to be understood deeply, they must not merely be passively received but must be worked on by the student, thought about, reasoned with and discussed with others.*

Fluency – Quick and efficient recall of facts and procedures and the flexibility to move between different contexts and representations of mathematics.

Variation – Variation is twofold. It is firstly about how the teacher represents the concept being taught, often in more than one way, to draw attention to critical aspects, and to develop deep and holistic understanding. It is also about the sequencing of the episodes, activities and exercises used within a lesson and follow up practice, paying attention to what is kept the same and what changes, to connect the mathematics and draw attention to mathematical relationships and structure.

(NCETM, 2017)

While this is not statutory, the term 'mastery', its associated practices in mathematics and its alignment to statutory provision are certainly ubiquitous across primary schools in England today, and the NCETM is now expanding its materials and provision to target Early Years settings.

ACTIVITY

Highlight keywords and phrases in each of the above extracts (The EYFS, ELGs, the NCETM's definition of 'mastery' and their '5 Big Ideas').

Identify any similarities. Which words or ideas appear in more than one extract?

Identify any contradictions or tensions. What questions do you have?

REFLECTION

Can you identify any features of practice that you have observed or enacted that you consider to be examples of any of these ideas?

EXPLORING NON-STATUTORY GUIDANCE

The 'Development Matters' (DfE, 2021b) document offers non-statutory curriculum guidance for the EYFS, and with regard to mathematics specific examples of what children might be learning and how this might be supported are offered across three progressive age bands: 0–3 years, 3–4 years and Children in Reception (p. 86–98).

Department
for Education

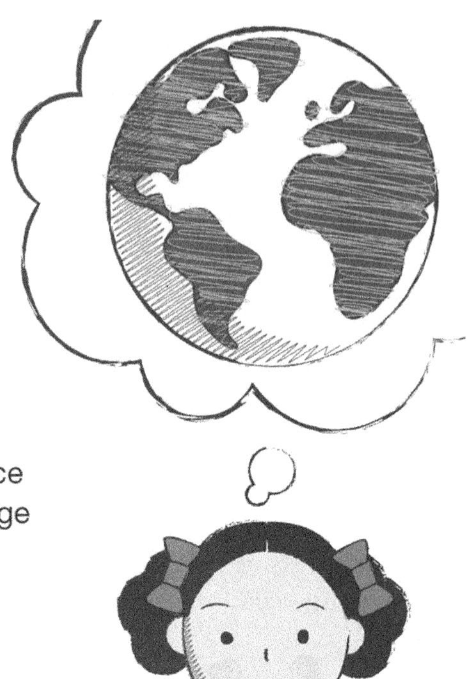

Development Matters

Non-statutory curriculum guidance
for the early years foundation stage

First published September 2020
Revised July 2021

Figure 1.3

As might be expected, the suggested progression focuses on the content knowledge and skills of the EYFS, namely number, shape, space, measure and pattern. The more behavioural aspects of mathematical development are implicit in the broader characteristics of effective teaching and learning listed in the statutory documentation:

- playing and exploring – children investigate and experience things, and 'have a go';
- active learning – children concentrate and keep on trying if they encounter difficulties, and enjoy achievements;
- creating and thinking critically – children have and develop their own ideas, make links between ideas, and develop strategies for doing things.

'Birth to 5 Matters' (Early Years Coalition, 2021) provides support for Early Years educators to 'implement the Statutory Framework for the Early Years Foundation Stage (EYFS) in a pedagogically sound, principled and evidence-based way' (paragraph 3, https://birthto5matters.org.uk/background/) and was created by a coalition of the UK's 16 Early Years sector organisations.

From the beginning, this document states that its strands of learning do not precisely match those found in the ELGs, as the developers have prioritised aligning their guidance with holistic child development and broader curriculum content. The ELGs for 'number' and 'numerical patterns' are therefore incorporated into the broader strand of 'mathematics' which, similarly to 'development matters' retains emphasis on shape, space and measure. One way in which 'Birth to 5 Matters' differs from 'Development Matters' is in its use of *ranges* as stages of progression. This is intended to acknowledge and provide support for navigating non-linear and unpredictable mathematical development, and to avoid a pre-determined path according to a standardised age-related expectation. In this way, the 'Birth to 5 Matters' document and resources endeavours to support practitioners to keep the unique child at the centre of their practice. Across the six ranges, it also signposts practitioners to specific areas of mathematical learning through subheadings which (alongside number, shape, measures and pattern) include spatial awareness, cardinality, comparison, counting and composition. Associated resources on the affiliated website offer a useful glossary for these terms.

The Education Endowment Foundation (EEF) is an independent charity that works to summarise and disseminate educational research in formats that are useful to and accessible for practitioners and teachers. Their guidance report on 'Improving Mathematics in the Early Years and Key Stage One' (2020) makes five key recommendations for practice:

1. Develop practitioners' understanding of how children learn mathematics
2. Dedicate time for children to learn mathematics and integrate mathematics throughout the day
3. Use manipulatives and representations to develop understanding
4. Ensure that teaching builds on what children already know
5. Use high-quality targeted support to help all children learn mathematics.

The report breaks down each of these recommendations into key definitions, examples of practice, case studies and further reading/resources to support developments in professional practice.

ACTIVITY

Take some time to explore the mathematics guidance and resources of 'Development Matters', 'Birth to 5 Matters' and the EEF.

Note the similarities and identify any differences. Which (parts) do you find most useful? Why?

WHAT DOES OFSTED SAY ABOUT EARLY MATHEMATICAL LEARNING?

Ofsted's (2021) 'Research Review Series: Mathematics' offers the inspectorate's analysis of a range of research and its potential application to the teaching and learning of mathematics across 'all age groups including Reception year'. It concludes that success is engineered through 'systems thinking' approaches which are observable as:

- detailed codification and sequencing of the facts, methods and strategies that pupils will acquire;
- instructional coherence and aligned rehearsal that increase the chances of understanding and remembering while minimising the need for guesswork or trial and error.

These, and other more specific conclusions reached throughout the review, prioritise the transmission of knowledge through textbooks, memorisation through practice and its part in the development of conceptual understanding and procedural fluency, as well as highlighting that lower-quality mathematics education is likely to have gaps in content, instruction, rehearsal and assessment. This is one of the documents that has influenced a growing sector-wide concern about the potentially narrowing and restrictive view of mathematics that it seems to advocate.

Similarly, these themes are evident as part of another widely debated document, Ofsted's (2017) 'Bold Beginnings' which focused on practice in Reception, classifying this as a 'unique and important year' and therefore seeming to separate this later phase of the EYFS for 4–5-year-olds which often happens in a school setting. In the schools that were deemed 'most effective' and therefore included in the sample, the following practices were prioritised:

- the direct teaching of the whole class, with sufficient time to practise and rehearse important processes and skills;
- a whole school 'teaching for mastery' approach to mathematics;
- the use of practical activities and equipment, giving young children materials to manipulate to aid their understanding and lay the foundations for visual images that represent numbers;
- counting, numeral recognition and the additive composition of number as the prerequisites for later, more complex mathematical concepts;
- traditional games, at school and at home, that enabled children to apply their counting and hone their early calculation skills.

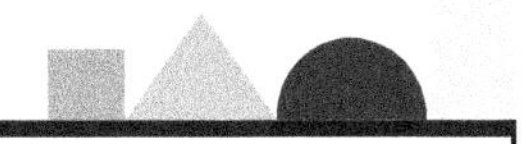

ACTIVITY

Identify similarities and differences between the Ofsted (2021) research review and the Ofsted (2017) Bold beginnings document.

Note down the key points about Ofsted's view of early mathematical learning.

Is anything missing? If so, what?

Does this reflect your views on and experiences of early mathematics?

In their published response to Ofsted's (2021) research review, the Early Childhood Maths Group (ECMG) (2021), a 'UK-based group of Early Years mathematics enthusiasts and experts', endorses some of these key messages, particularly those referring to systematic planning and the importance of the role of the adult. However, they highlight that the review is unclear in both its definition of 'young learners' and its misrepresentation of specific research evidence which appears to advocate a necessity for a highly instructional 'teacher' adult and a reductive view of the value of games and 'informal' procedures. The Joint Primary ATM and MA Group, drawn from two subject associations (the Association of Teachers of Mathematics and the Mathematical Association), also published a response to the review which translates each of the Ofsted recommendations into 'a practical guide for the classroom practitioner' including reference to Early Years (2021). The document provides links to further reading, summaries of what each point could 'look like' in practice, examples from the classroom and links to relevant supportive materials.

We will return to some of the themes from these documents when we consider 'Transition to Key Stage One' in Chapter 9.

The Ofsted view of the role of the adult in Early Years is more explicitly explored, although not with specific reference to mathematics, in 'Teaching and Play in the Early Years – a balancing act?' (2015). This document has a different approach to Early Years practice than that taken in the subsequent 'Bold Beginnings' document and therefore highlights some contradictions in Ofsted's evolving position. They acknowledge that the role of the adult in Early Years education was not talked about by all those they spoke to using the same terms; 'practitioner', 'teacher' and 'educator' were all used, with some making the distinction of themselves as 'not a teacher' due to their lack of Qualified Teacher Status (QTS). Although it was also acknowledged that 'teaching' was largely used as an overarching term to encompass the provision of opportunities for learning in their entirety. Some made a distinction between 'adult-led' and 'child-led' learning, classifying the first as 'teaching' and the second as 'play' and a further classification of the former as 'formal' and related to the 'transmission of knowledge'. However, in contrast to messages found in the Research

Review Series: Mathematics (Ofsted, 2021), this report is clear on its definition of teaching in the Early Years:

> *Teaching should not be taken to imply a 'top down' or formal way of working. It is a broad term which covers the many different ways in which adults help young children learn. It includes their interactions with children during planned and child-initiated play and activities: communicating and modelling language, showing, explaining, demonstrating, exploring ideas, encouraging, questioning, recalling, providing a narrative for what they are doing, facilitating and setting challenges. It takes account of the equipment they provide and the attention to the physical environment as well as the structure and routines of the day that establish expectations. Integral to teaching is how practitioners assess what children know, understand and can do as well as take account of their interests and dispositions to learning (characteristics of effective learning), and use this information to plan children's next steps in learning and monitor their progress.*
>
> (Ofsted, 2015, p. 11)

The term 'guided learning' has increased in usage since the introduction of the new EYFS (DfE, 2021a), and this is the term we will use when referring to planned mathematical interactions in the Early Years/Reception.

ACTIVITY

Identify the words and phrases used to define 'teaching' in the extract above. Which of these do you use in mathematical learning in your setting?

To what extent does Ofsted's (2015) definition cover what you see as your role?

Ofsted (2015) also recognise that mathematical subject knowledge and confidence to teach were higher for those working in Reception than for those in 'pre-school' settings working with 2–4-year-olds due to levels of qualifications, training and personal experiences of learning mathematics. They identify this as worthy of note as, within a high-quality Early Years provision the ability to capitalise on opportunities for mathematical learning is reliant on highly attuned and mathematically useful responses to children's starting points that enhance, rather than stifle, their thinking – whether or not the adult is present.

SUMMARY

As you can see, many factors are currently influencing Early Years practice as part of the context(s) surrounding mathematics education in the UK. The EYFS, ELGs, the

NCETM's 'mastery approach', 'Development Matters', 'Birth to 5 Matters', the EEF and Ofsted all contribute to a landscape that encompasses both coherence and contradiction which, whether we are conscious of it or not, influences the parameters within which we work, and the choices we make in our settings and schools. Common to all of these sources is the belief that effective mathematics teaching in the Early Years is essential to enable children to develop the strong foundations on which to build their subsequent mathematical learning and understanding. There is a (potentially overwhelming!) plethora of books, websites, resources, schemes, advice, guidance and opinions to be accessed, experimented with and evaluated as we work to embed high-quality mathematical learning for all the children in our care. Through this book, we aim to offer a framework incorporating key principles of practice that we hope will be useful to all adults who work with children in the Early Years phase to develop their ability to identify and develop effective and enjoyable 'teachable moments' (Ofsted, 2015, p. 9) for all involved.

FURTHER READING/RESOURCES

East Midlands West Maths Hub. (2017). *Mastery in early years*. http://emwest.co.uk/wp-content/uploads/2017/04/Mastery-in-Early-Years-Booklet.pdf

Joint ATM and MA Primary Group. (2021). *Responding to the 2021 mathematics Ofsted research review: A practical guide for the classroom practitioner*. https://www.atm.org.uk/write/MediaUploads/ATM%20News/ATM_MA_FINAL_Response_to_Ofsted_Research_Review-links.pdf

NCETM. (2022). *Early years*. https://www.ncetm.org.uk/in-the-classroom/early-years/

Nrich. (2022). *Early years foundation stage homepage*. https://nrich.maths.org/early-years

REFERENCES

DfE. (2021a). *Statutory framework for the early years foundation stage setting the standards for learning, development and care for children from birth to five*. https://assets.publishing.service.gov.uk/government/uploads/system/uploads/attachment_data/file/974907/EYFS_framework_-_March_2021.pdf

DfE. (2021b). *Development matters non-statutory curriculum guidance for the early years foundation stage*. https://assets.publishing.service.gov.uk/government/uploads/system/uploads/attachment_data/file/988004/Development_Matters.pdf

Early Years Coalition. (2021). *Birth to 5 Matters: Non-statutory guidance for the early years foundation stage.* https://www.birthto5matters.org.uk/

ECMG. (2021). *Letter to Ofsted.* https://earlymaths.org/wp-content/uploads/2021/07/ECMG-letter-to-Ofsted-July-2021.pdf

Education Endowment Fund. (2020). *Improving mathematics in the early years and KS1.* https://educationendowmentfoundation.org.uk/public/files/Publications/Maths/EEF_Maths_EY_KS1_Guidance_Report.pdf

Joint ATM and MA Primary Group. (2021). *Responding to the 2021 mathematics Ofsted research review: A practical guide for the classroom practitioner.* https://www.atm.org.uk/write/MediaUploads/ATM%20News/ATM_MA_FINAL_Response_to_Ofsted_Research_Review-links.pdf

NCETM. (2017). *Five big ideas in teaching for mastery.* https://www.ncetm.org.uk/teaching-for-mastery/mastery-explained/five-big-ideas-in-teaching-for-mastery/

NCETM. (2022). *Mastery explained.* https://www.ncetm.org.uk/teaching-for-mastery/mastery-explained/

Ofsted. (2015). *Teaching and play in the early years – balancing act.* https://assets.publishing.service.gov.uk/government/uploads/system/uploads/attachment_data/file/936086/Teaching-and-play-in-the-early-years-a-balancing-act.pdf

Ofsted. (2017). *Bold beginnings: The reception curriculum in a sample of good and outstanding primary schools.* https://assets.publishing.service.gov.uk/government/uploads/system/uploads/attachment_data/file/663560/28933_Ofsted_-_Early_Years_Curriculum_Report_-_Accessible.pdf

Ofsted. (2021). *Research review series: Mathematics.* https://www.gov.uk/government/publications/research-review-series-mathematics/research-review-series-mathematics#conclusion

2

WHAT MATTERS (MOST) IN EARLY MATHEMATICS?

CHAPTER OBJECTIVES

- Consider the purpose of mathematics education, and how this influences early mathematical learning
- Increase awareness of a range of purposes and the choices open to Early Years educators when responding to children's mathematics

INTRODUCTION

We can approach the question of what matters in early mathematical learning in a variety of ways. We could list elements of knowledge that can be identified as forming the foundations for later mathematical learning. We could explore ideas about the cognitive growth of young children and how to nurture their aptitude to 'think mathematically'. We could discuss the mathematical culture and environment that surrounds and influences each child's development. Whichever path we choose may inevitably lead us into others as these starting points are not mutually exclusive and necessarily overlap but, before we choose a path, perhaps we need to think about where it is we are heading. Perhaps a more fundamental question that we need to find our answers to, before we can make decisions about what *matters* at any stage of learning, is 'What is mathematics *for?*'.

The National Curriculum 'Purpose of Study' statement lists several potential answers to this question, it is 'essential to everyday life, critical to science, technology, and engineering, and necessary for financial literacy and most forms of employment' (DfE, 2013, p. 99). Herein we can see themes of utility and function; mathematics serves a purpose as it provides humans with the skills and knowledge necessary to attain the resources needed for everyday life. This is a pervasive view of the purpose of mathematics, held by many of the students and teachers with whom we work, who offer valid justifications rooted in ideas of equality and inclusivity. Indeed, the view that mathematics is both a vehicle for and prerequisite of social justice is widespread. As a 'gatekeeper subject', access to employment and further education can be granted or denied based on exam results, therefore access to economic stability is inextricably bound to mathematical competence at school, and it follows that the ability to access resources such as food and housing are a consequence of this. Even for those members of our society who might not be able to reach conventional standards of mathematical attainment in terms of exams, the mathematical ability needed to successfully shop for and cook food must at least be a desirable outcome for maths education.

The National Curriculum does not stop there though. It goes on to state that mathematics education 'provides a foundation for understanding the world, the ability to reason mathematically, an appreciation of the beauty and power of mathematics, and a sense of enjoyment and curiosity about the subject' (DfE, 2013, p. 99). Here the purpose of learning mathematics is broader, more far-reaching and philosophical than the functionality of the preceding statements. It encompasses more ethereal and abstract ideas concerned with making sense of the world and human experience, and acknowledges the feelings of human beings towards the subject as something that has value and purpose in and of itself. While most students and teachers are comfortable with mathematics' potential to support our ability to *think* and *understand*, and even that mathematical enquiry might be motivating and even enjoyable, the idea that it has beauty and power often causes sometimes incredulous but often thoughtful, debate.

ACTIVITY

Name as many mathematicians as you can. What do you think they do/did?

(Before reading on...!) What do you predict they would say about what maths is for?

WHAT DO MATHEMATICIANS SAY?

What do mathematicians believe?

We believe math is interesting, true, and useful (in that order).

> *We believe in a process called "mathematical proof." We believe the knowledge produced by proof is important and powerful.*
>
> *Fundamentalist mathematicians believe that everything – plants, love, music, everything – can (in theory) be understood in terms of math.*
>
> (Beckman, 2021)

Benjamin (2013) outlines three core purposes for the learning of mathematics, 'calculation, application and inspiration...including, perhaps, the most important application of all, learning how to think'. This notion of learning how to think goes beyond thinking *about* mathematics as a rich mathematical education enables learners to 'become more resistant to the pressure of propaganda, more critical in their own thinking, and more intelligent in meeting the responsibilities of citizenship' (Fawcett, 1947, p. 205). Even more profoundly, when asked, 'Why do mathematics?', Su (2020) responds, 'Mathematics helps people flourish. Mathematics is for human flourishing' (p. 10).

BEAUTY MATTERS

Mathematics is everywhere in the natural and man-made design of the world around us, and children are surrounded by its beauty from birth. Symmetry, pattern and the structures that form their foundations are visible in faces, their own bodies, and their immediate environment from the first moments that they open their eyes. Mathematical beauty appears in two forms: generic beauty which has an abstracted, awe-inspiring effect as we notice commonalities and order; and exceptional beauty which delights in disruptions to that order, the unpredicted, quirky misfits, or special cases (Dijkgraaf, 2020) (Figures 2.1 and 2.2).

Developing our awareness of these occurrences of beauty, and their inherent 'mathematicalness' can help us to enhance children's understanding of and appreciation for both the world around them and their own creations. Opportunities and experiences that draw on and promote geometrical and artistic activity such as playing with pattern blocks, Cuisenaire rods, 3D shapes (including more unusual examples from packaging), building blocks, tiles, collage, K'nex©, Clixi© etc. are all potentially beautiful (Figures 2.3 and 2.4).

We might introduce the vocabulary of symmetry, repetition, growing patterns, fractals, the golden spiral and see where the children's curiosity takes them (and us!) in ever-deepening wonder at the beauty of mathematics.

Figure 2.1 Buildings inspired by nature. The lotus temple in India, inspired by the lotus flower; the Beijing national stadium in China, inspired by birds' nests; the Olympic pavilion in Barcelona, Spain, inspired by fish; and the Eastgate development in Zimbabwe, inspired by termite structures. (Online version in colour). (Adapted from Perera & Coppens, 2018, p.3)

> *To those who do not know mathematics it is difficult to get across a real feeling as to the beauty, the deepest beauty, of nature ... If you want to learn about nature, to appreciate nature, it is necessary to understand the language that she speaks in.*
>
> (Feynman, 1967)

Figure 2.2 Examples of patterns in nature, including the golden spiral, the golden ratio, and fractal self-similar structures. From left to right, (a) a nautilus shell, a galaxy, a sunflower, a desert plant; (b) a storm formation, a fern bud, an ocean wave, a finger print; (c) fractal properties in a branched tree, a leaf, river bed formation, a cast of human lungs (Online version in colour) (Perera & Coppens, 2018, p. 7)

Figure 2.3 https://en.unesco.org/news/comoros-celebrates-international-day-islamic-art-promote-cultural-diversity-and-status-artists, http://g1-27originaldesign.blogspot.com/2014/12/sheily-rose-new-pattern-block-design.html

Figure 2.4

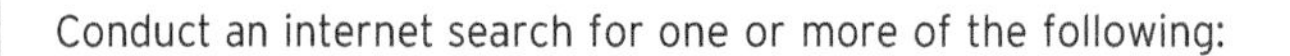

ACTIVITY

Conduct an internet search for one or more of the following:

- The Golden Ratio
- Fractals
- Maths in Nature
- Maths in Art

Collect some examples of mathematical beauty and make a display in your setting – how many examples of beauty can you find in one day?

THINKING MATTERS

The core foundations of mathematical thinking can be listed as:

- Exploring
- Questioning
- Working systematically
- Visualising
- Conjecturing
- Explaining
- Generalising
- Justifying
- Proving

(Nrich, 2020)

ACTIVITY

Define and give examples of each of the above words. What do each of them 'look like' for the children in your setting? Are they always/only identifiable in 'maths-y' activity? To what extent are they related to the Early Years' Characteristics of Effective Learning ('playing and exploring'; 'active learning'; 'creative and critical thinking')?

We wonder how many of your definitions and examples refer to, either explicitly or implicitly, the 'structures' and 'connections' that form part of the beauty of mathematics? Perhaps in 'working systematically' you are referring to ideas of 'what comes next...?' or in 'visualising' there is a sense of how parts fit together, or in 'conjecturing' there are connections between ideas, 'If I know...then I know...'. In asking children to pay attention to these elements and engage in activities that provoke the behaviours listed above, we are often prompting them to re-evaluate and extend their prior knowledge and ideas and so are prioritising what they will be *thinking* above what they will be *doing* (Tyler, 2021). The testing of whether or not new knowledge makes sense is a core element of the Primary National Curriculum embodied in the aim of 'reasoning'. The questions and prompts that we employ during such activities can also form an integral element of developing mathematical thinking (Jeffcoat et al., 2004) – an idea we will return to in chapter 6 'How are we talking?'

Nrich (2020) also identify mathematical 'habits of mind' that are essential to support the development of mathematical thinking: curiosity, collaboration, resourcefulness and resilience. If we want young children to become confident and competent mathematicians, then the learning culture we create in our settings forms the foundation on which these habits of mind can be nurtured to grow. Watson's (2021a) identification of 'care' in mathematics, particularly in terms of 'care for mathematics' and 'care for learning through relationships' is particularly relevant to this. She argues that there are key facets of practice that contribute to this caring culture:

- the absence of 'talking at' and the primacy of 'listening to'; response to students' ideas, language and sense-making; adapting teaching to support learning;
- working with what students bring into the educational space; incorporating students' emotional and social selves in mathematics learning; treating students as individuals within wider society and communities;
- design and choice of tasks that support meaning-making; using multiple materials and representations; using 'outside' as a source for mathematising;
- expectations of and support for capabilities of abstract reasoning; teachers and students working side by side on mathematical tasks;
- curriculum norms being respected, but students' interests and strengths often take priority (p. 80).

The strong foundation of a physically and emotionally safe (enabling) environment in which mathematical thinking can thrive relies upon opportunities to use intuition and the confidence to explore mistakes as a natural part of the learning process (Gifford, 2015) as part of rich interactions and shared thinking over time (Williams, 2021). As Watson (2021b) states, there is a need to create time for learners' thinking and the consideration of different ideas which is 'more than the slowing down of content coverage...It is the slowing down required for the teacher to listen. It is giving priority to the learners and their learning, not to the planned teaching' (p. 14).

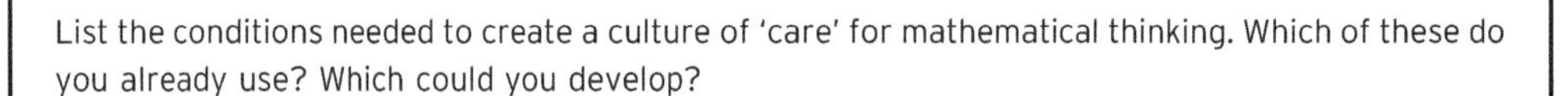

ACTIVITY

List the conditions needed to create a culture of 'care' for mathematical thinking. Which of these do you already use? Which could you develop?

CONTENT MATTERS

Again, we see ideas of pattern and structure forming key elements of early mathematical content. In their resource materials to help Early Years providers, the DfE (2021) interprets the EYFS framework to prioritise three areas: numbers, patterns and connections, and spatial reasoning. The NCETM (2022) distinguish six key areas of early mathematics learning: cardinality and counting, comparison, composition, pattern, shape and space, and measures, the first three of which explicitly relate to the teaching of number. When considering *what matters* in terms of specific subject content, the idea of core or foundational knowledge that underpins subsequent mathematical curricula throughout primary and beyond is a key driver. Metaphors of mathematics that include elements of building blocks or linear pathways where each 'step' is dependent on the security of the one before it reflect this view of mathematics.

However, there must be a cautionary note with regard to the consequential pressure that could arise for specific listed sub-elements of content to be sufficiently 'covered' by the end of the EYFS for all children. There is a potential risk that such coverage could result in superficial performance of key ideas that is not embedded into children's understanding, and subsequently is forgotten. In order to counteract this, attention must be paid to the mathematical concepts that relate smaller parts of knowledge content into a bigger conceptual picture (Myatt, 2022), leading to deeper and more connected mathematical understanding. The specific content covered by both the EYFS and the NCETM materials is explored in more detail in Chapter 3, and the ways in which we might support connections between concepts and content is explored further in Chapter 8.

SUMMARY

Whatever we think mathematics is *for* will influence our prioritisation of what *matters*. Valuing the learning of mathematics as something that offers a broader view of an inspirational window to **beauty** and power might lead us to foreground learning about mathematics in nature, architecture, art or the humanities and the subject's inherent elegance. If the idea of developing **thinking** resonates more, we might prioritise pedagogy and 'application' activities that facilitate enquiry and discussion in an intellectually safe environment. A stronger alignment with the usefulness and function of mathematics might lead us to focus on teaching **content** knowledge that develops an aptitude for calculation and the application of specific skills in 'real-life'. Of course, we may shift between and across each of these as elements of a rounded education over time and dependent on context.

Children will have innumerable opportunities to explore many aspects of mathematics through their early experiences and play. They will build block towers and junk models. They will block paint and explore symmetry creating butterfly pictures. They will run their own shops and bake cakes, both deliciously edible and more figurative examples in a mud kitchen or sandpit! Whether the mathematics is formally explored with the children or not, all children come to the setting with mathematical knowledge. This provides the initial building blocks for exploration. It is the role of the effective educator to nurture and develop mathematical understanding from those experiences; explore what a child does know, how that fits within the curriculum expectations, to identify any misconceptions and to consider how to progress the learning. As Su (2020) states, *'every single one of us, whether we realize it or not, is a teacher of math'* (p. 9, original emphasis), and there is an inextricable link between what we consider *matters* and what we *value* in the offerings of our mathematical learners. The next chapter gives you the opportunity to explore how you can develop your understanding of what matter for *you* as you grow your mathematical confidence in both teaching and life.

FURTHER READING/RESOURCES

Nrich. (2020). *Thinking mathematically.* https://nrich.maths.org/mathematically

Williams, H. (2018). *Mathematics in the early years: What matters?* Impact: Chartered College. https://my.chartered.college/impact_article/mathematics-in-the-early-years-what-matters/

Woo, E. (2018). *Eddie Woo: How math is our real sixth sense.* TEDxSydney.

REFERENCES

Beckman, M. (2021). *Math without numbers.* Penguin.

Benjamin, A. (2013). *Arthur Benjamin: The magic of Fibonacci numbers.* TEDGlobal2013.

DfE. (2013). *The national curriculum in England key stages 1 and 2 framework document.* https://assets.publishing.service.gov.uk/government/uploads/system/uploads/attachment_data/file/425601/PRIMARY_national_curriculum.pdf

DfE. (2021). *Help for early years providers: Mathematics.* https://help-for-early-years-providers.education.gov.uk/mathematics

Dijkgraaf, R. (2020). The two forms of mathematical beauty. *Quanta Magazine.* https://www.quantamagazine.org/how-is-math-beautiful-20200616/

Fawcett, H. (1947). Mathematics for responsible citizenship. *The Mathematics Teacher, 40*(5), 199–205. National Council of Teachers of Mathematics.

Feynman, R. (1967). *The character of physical laws.* MIT Press.

Gifford, S. (2015). *Early years mathematics: How to create a nation of mathematics lovers?* NRICH. https://nrich.maths.org/11441

Jeffcoat, M., Jones, M., Mansergh, J., Mason, J., Sewell, H., & Watson, A. (2004). *Primary questions and prompts for mathematical thinking.* ATM.

Myatt, M. (2022). *The curse of content coverage.* https://www.marymyatt.com/blog/the-curse-of-content-coverage

NCETM. (2022). *Early years.* https://www.ncetm.org.uk/in-the-classroom/early-years/

Nrich. (2022). *Thinking mathematically.* https://nrich.maths.org/mathematically

Perera, A., & Coppens, M.-O. (2018). *Re-designing materials for biomedical applications: From biomimicry to nature-inspired chemical engineering.* The Royal Society Publishing.

Su, F. (2020). *Mathematics for human flourishing.* Yale University Press.

Tyler, L. (2021). *Ofsted's research review: Standing on the shoulders of (maths) giants?* Arl Curriculum Plus. https://www.arkcurriculumplus.org.uk/news-events/4-ofsteds-research-review-standing-on-the-shoulders-of-maths-giants

Watson, A. (2021a). *Care in mathematics education.* Basingstoke: Palgrave Macmillan.

Watson, A. (2021b). *Care, Mathematics Teaching, 279,* 11–15. ATM.

Williams, H. (2021). *Mathematics in the early years: What matters?* Ponderings on Maths Education. https://info125328.wixsite.com/website/post/mathematics-in-the-early-years-what-matters

3

MATHS AND YOU

CHAPTER OBJECTIVES

- Consider the importance of your relationship with mathematics
- Explore key ideas of mathematical subject-matter knowledge, pedagogical content knowledge and curriculum knowledge
- Consider key subject-matter knowledge for effective teaching and learning of mathematics in the Reception year

INTRODUCTION

Through our many years working with both trainees and established Early Years educators, we have been made aware that mathematics is a subject often dreaded and rarely loved! We have frequently been told that Early Years teaching was a career choice in part because of the lower levels of mathematics involved. We know these are not the views of all Early Years educators and, even when said out loud, they do not tell the whole picture. However, they do reveal a pervading idea that maths in the Early Years is in some ways not as important as it becomes later in a child's schooling. The views we hold are influential to the way we approach teaching and learning in mathematics (Anderson et al., 2018; Boaler, 2014), so in this chapter we want to recognise and champion the importance of establishing strong foundations for future mathematics learning in the Early Years and consider how our relationship with mathematics influences us in achieving this. To consider these ideas, three key themes are explored; the importance of reflecting on your relationship with mathematics, establishing solid foundations and building your own mathematical knowledge and confidence.

As we consider the importance of your own relationship with mathematics, we draw on our experiences working with both trainee and established Early Years educators to explore beliefs about both the subject itself and how it is learnt effectively. We identify and unpick some anxieties that relate to both the teaching and learning of mathematics. Then, in order to establish solid foundations for our exploration of effective teaching and learning in mathematics, we refer to the Knowledge Quartet framework, developed by Rowland et al. (2009). We outline the framework and key theory that underpins it, exploring the key features of different aspects of mathematical subject knowledge; *subject-matter knowledge, pedagogical content knowledge and curriculum knowledge.* This chapter concludes with a section focusing on building and developing your own subject–matter knowledge alongside recognising common misconceptions. In this section, the core aspects of mathematics that children will be learning in the Reception class will be examined and explained in relation to key teaching and learning points. There will also be resources signposted that can further support personal mathematical development.

THE IMPORTANCE OF YOUR RELATIONSHIP WITH MATHEMATICS

ACTIVITY

'Maths is...'

If you were to complete this sentence with just one word, what would it be?

Over the years we have asked this question to many student teachers. The word cloud below shows the responses of a cohort of undergraduate teachers at the start of their first-year core maths module (Figure 3.1).

We generally find the words fall into three categories. Firstly, there are words from people who clearly have a positive relationship with mathematics; words such as 'beautiful', 'interesting', 'fun' or 'exciting'. Then, there are the practical answers; maths is 'useful', 'numbers', 'problem-solving' and so forth. Finally, there are words from those who have a more negative relationship with the subject. Maths is 'boring', 'difficult', 'terrifying' or 'upsetting'. You will recognise some of the key themes from the previous chapter coming through in the word choices. The important thing to

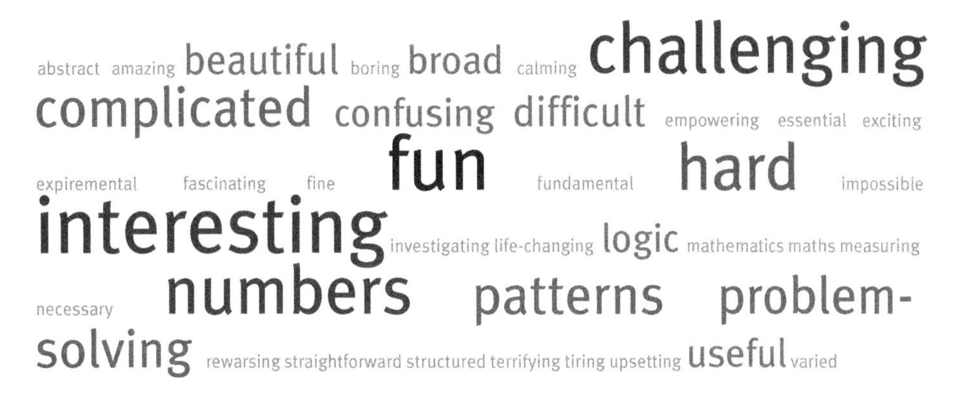

Figure 3.1 'Maths is...' words from our year one cohort

note is that nobody is born with these opinions. We do not have an inbuilt switch that decides if we are maths lovers, maths haters or can merely see its value for practical use and application. These conclusions develop over time and come through our experiences as learners, our conversations with those we look up to and the attitudes of our role models. The combination of all these aspects, and many more, will lead us to summarise maths using our one chosen word.

ACTIVITY

Before going any further we invite you to reflect on your own experiences of mathematics.

- On a blank sheet of paper, draw and label a timeline of your maths journey so far. Try to remember your first mathematical memory, then fill in any others that lead to where you are now reading this book!
- Don't think of this as an end point though; What questions do you have as you look forward to continuing your journey? Is there anything you want to achieve in your future mathematical journey?
- How do you feel about teaching maths and recognising spontaneous teachable moments in an Early Years environment?

REFLECTION

Now spend some time considering the answers to the following questions relating to the journey you have just drawn.

- What have you chosen to include? Why?

(Continued)

(Continued)

- What were the high points? Why were these high points? How could you ensure learners in your care have similar positive experiences?
- What were the low points? Why were these low points? How could you ensure learners in your care do not have similar negative experiences?

Your relationship with mathematics is important, which is why it is essential to spend time reflecting on your current attitudes towards maths and where your ideas and beliefs may have come from. A role model who is positive and enthusiastic about maths, someone who does not need to have all the answers but is open to exploring and playing with maths, will inspire a class to have a similar attitude towards maths. Someone who is anxious or holds a negative attitude towards the subject will probably unintentionally shut down maths exploration, missing opportunities and not realising the potential for maths in play and exploration. In turn, this will limit the children's experiences and expectations of the subject.

As educators we need to recognise and care about the importance of mathematics as both a practical and a beautiful subject while also understanding how developing mathematical thinking can have much wider implications for learning in other subjects. We also need to recognise and care about the importance of nurturing a positive attitude towards it in all learners. This care can then have an important impact on our classroom practices. As Watson (2021, p. 11) explains, 'Care is an enactment of love, but what is more useful is that care can be a sequence of actions, need not become locked up as a frustration of feelings, and is less susceptible to misinterpretation than "love". If I care for mathematics, I am less likely to degrade it for the sake of expedience; if I care for learners, I am less likely to crush them for the sake of conformity; if I care about mathematics and learners, it is more likely that my students will care. If I care about bringing the two together, I am less likely to follow instructions blindly if they might degrade mathematics and crush learners.'

Whatever your attitude towards mathematics as you initially read this chapter, we firmly believe that everyone has the potential to be a fantastic teacher of mathematics.

- If you are coming with a passion for the subject you will naturally want to share this, looking for ways to explore mathematical ideas, make connections and communicate your enthusiasm for the subject.
- If you are coming with a level of dislike for the subject, you will know how this can have an impact on your motivation and perhaps confidence, so you will recognise the importance of ensuring no children in your care end up feeling like

this. Reflecting on your experiences will encourage you to teach maths in a different way to the way you were taught. You can focus on developing conceptual understanding, both for you and the children, so you can confidently explain ideas and concepts.

- If you recognise the practical application of mathematics, understanding purpose and contexts for learning will probably motivate your planning, ensuring children appreciate how prevalent it is in the world around them rather than an abstract subject that has no meaning further than the piece of paper it is written on.

Wherever you currently are, as your confidence and enthusiasm grow, you will take children on a mathematical exploration with you, ensuring they develop the secure foundations of mathematical learning that are so important in the Early Years. We hope this chapter will motivate and excite you to promote mathematical development enthusiastically and confidently through everyday play situations and guided learning.

SOLID FOUNDATIONS: THE KNOWLEDGE QUARTET FRAMEWORK

REFLECTION

What makes a good maths teacher?

What knowledge, skills, behaviours and beliefs does a good maths teacher need?

In this section of the chapter, we will examine these different aspects of being an effective maths teacher, exploring first the knowledge and skills required before considering the behaviours and beliefs.

KNOWLEDGE AND SKILLS

The considerations and structures we present for effective teaching and learning of mathematics are underpinned by Rowland et al.'s (2009) Knowledge Quartet. The following explanation of knowledge and skills is adapted from their explanations of key influences in the development of their work. When we think about teaching, Shulman (1986 cited in Rowland et al., 2009, p. 20) explains that there are seven types of knowledge teachers need to have. These are shown in the diagram below.

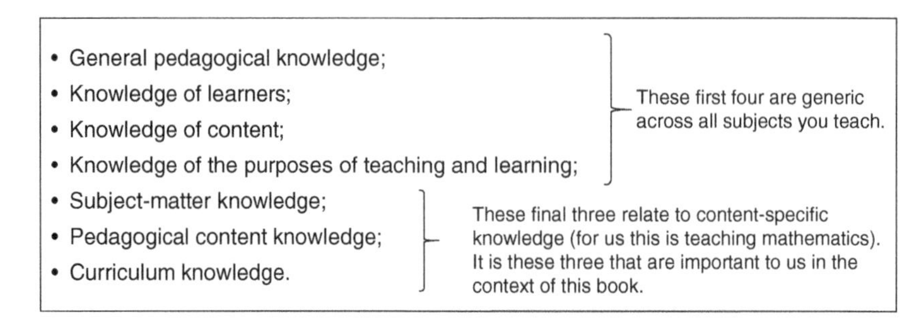

Figure 3.2 Types of knowledge needed for teaching

As shown in Figure 3.2, the first four types of knowledge are generic across all subjects and areas you teach. It is the final three that are content specific, in our case the teaching of mathematics. We now go on to explore each of the final three types of knowledge in more depth, from a mathematical perspective.

SUBJECT-MATTER KNOWLEDGE

This consists of two different types of knowledge:

- The first of these is **substantive knowledge**. This is knowledge about 'the facts, concepts and processes of mathematics and the links between them' (Rowland et al., 2009, p. 20). For example, this might be knowing the properties of a particular shape, understanding what is meant by halving, knowing number bonds to ten or understanding that addition and subtraction have an inverse relationship.
- The second is **syntactic knowledge**. This involves 'knowing how mathematical truths are established' and 'concerns the *process* of doing maths', rather than the outcomes (ibid, p. 21). Syntactic knowledge is about the process of enquiry in mathematics. 'It includes knowing how to *prove* an idea through deductive reasoning – for example being able to demonstrate why the sum of two odd numbers must be an even number. Another aspect of syntactic knowledge is knowing how to *disprove* a conjecture – for example, being able to use *counter-examples*' (ibid, p. 21). Consider the common misconception that multiplication always makes numbers bigger. Here we could find a simple counterexample, for instance, when we multiply by one the number in fact stays the same size. This ensures children are not surprised when later in their mathematical learning they are introduced to the idea that multiplying by a fraction makes a number smaller.

It is important to note that these two types of subject-matter knowledge are complimentary of each other rather than exclusive of each other. This is seen when looking at the mathematics overview in the Early Years Foundation Stage (EYFS) statutory framework (DfE, 2021, p. 10), which states:

> *Developing a strong grounding in number is essential so that all children develop the necessary building blocks to excel mathematically. Children should be able to count confidently, develop a deep understanding of the numbers to 10, the relationships between them and the patterns within those numbers. By providing frequent and varied opportunities to build and apply this understanding - such as using manipulatives, including small pebbles and tens frames for organising counting - children will develop a secure base of knowledge and vocabulary from which mastery of mathematics is built.*

While we clearly see the aim of developing children's substantive knowledge, this is underpinned by developing their syntactic knowledge by focusing on how these foundational ideas are developed and establishing a deep conceptual understanding of the structure and relationships within number.

PEDAGOGICAL CONTENT KNOWLEDGE

This type of knowledge is concerned with how a teacher transforms their own subject-matter knowledge so that it is accessible to learner. This includes knowledge of how to use concrete resources and pictorial representations to help develop children's conceptual understanding.

Look at the image of the Numicon showing number bonds to ten (Figure 3.3). While this might be the first aspect of mathematics you would consider when looking at this image, reflect on why this would also be an effective choice of manipulative when considering the earlier example of being able to demonstrate why the sum of two odd numbers must be an even number. There are many mathematical resources available and secure pedagogical knowledge will help you decide which is the most effective choice to model the idea or concept you are exploring. These ideas are explored in more depth in Chapter 5: Can we feel it and see it?

Figure 3.3 Numicon showing number bonds to ten

Pedagogical content knowledge is also concerned with 'how teachers break down ideas and explain concepts to learners' (Rowland et al., 2009, p. 21). We explore how this can be done effectively through a variety of lenses in Chapters 4–8.

CURRICULUM KNOWLEDGE

Curriculum knowledge is knowing what children are expected to learn and when they are expected to learn it. In our context this is the EYFS expectations of mathematics. As discussed in Chapter 1, the EYFS non-statutory documents, 'Development Matters' and 'Birth to 5 Matters', outline expected stages of development in relation to mathematical learning and understanding. This book has a focus on mathematical learning in the Reception year, but effective educators will want to be aware of the stages that come before the phase they are teaching and what the expectations are for the following year groups.

The Venn diagram below (Figure 3.4) shows how these different aspects of mathematical knowledge complement each other. The overlap in the centre represents the ideal combination of the three aspects, contributing to overall knowledge for teaching mathematics.

ACTIVITY

Reflect on your own knowledge for teaching mathematics. Are there any of these aspects that you consider to be stronger or any that would benefit from further development?

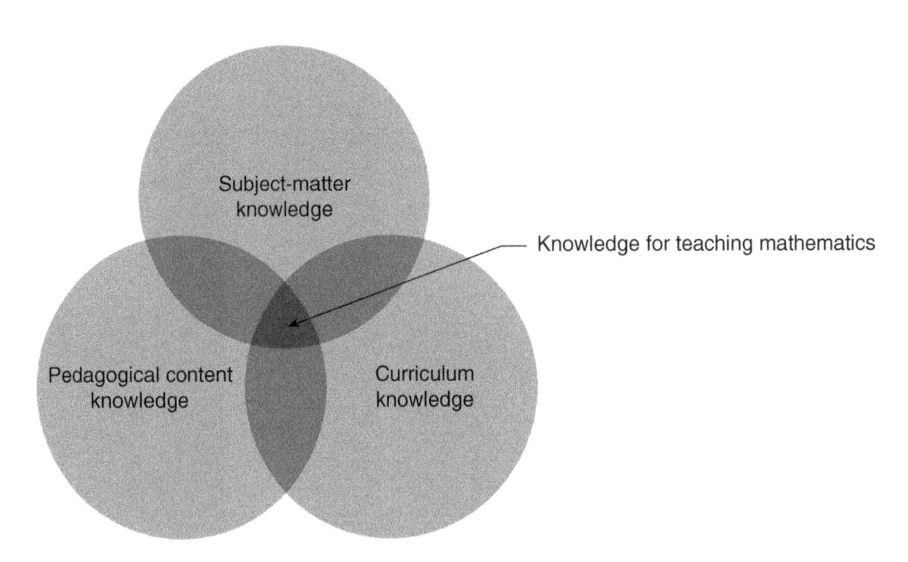

Figure 3.4 Overlap of the different types of knowledge for teaching mathematics

The 'Further Reading/Resources' section at the end of the chapter offers suggestions that may help develop different aspects of your knowledge for teaching mathematics. Developing all aspects of your own subject knowledge will increase your confidence for teaching mathematics, which in turn will motivate and inspire pupils' learning.

BEHAVIOUR AND BELIEFS

Consider the image below from the seminal work of Askew et al. (1997, p. 25), developed as part of the Effective Teachers of Numeracy report (Figure 3.5).

What is both striking and encouraging is the equal emphasis placed on 'teacher's beliefs' alongside their 'pedagogic content knowledge'. These both feed into 'teacher practices' and then on to 'pupil responses'. Later work by Boaler, who developed Dweck's work on mindsets for a mathematical context, also emphasises the importance of teachers' beliefs. One of Boaler's (no date) core principles is that 'everyone can learn maths to the highest levels.' It is interesting to reflect on your initial reaction to this statement. Is this something you believe and agree with, or is there a part of you that believes people are either 'maths people' or not?

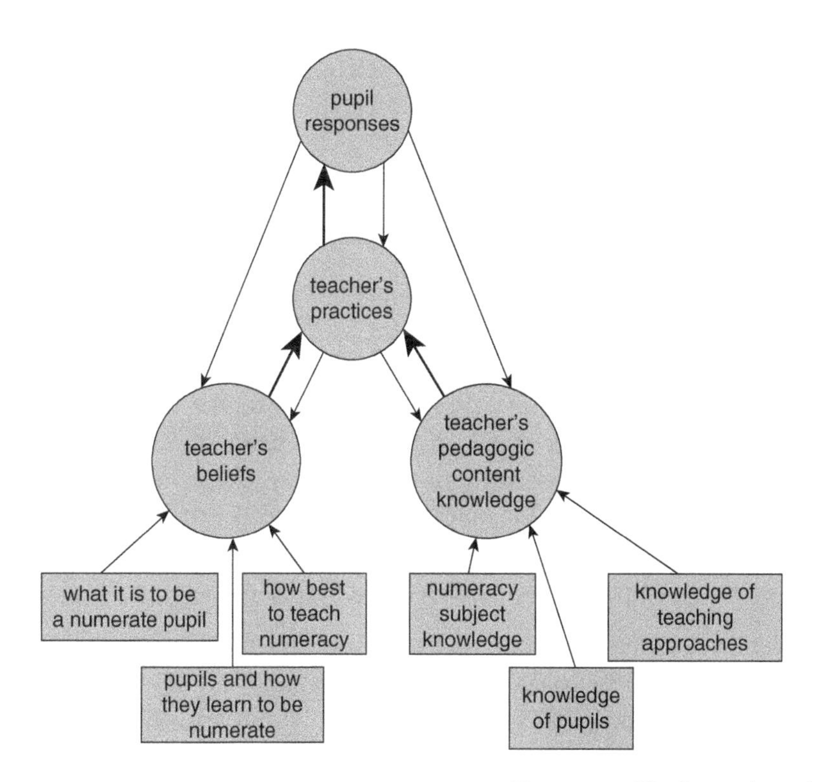

Figure 3.5 Effective teachers of numeracy

The myth of 'maths people' is potentially a damaging one, as it enables children to find an excuse to give up when they find the learning tricky or take longer to understand an idea than their friend or peers. Similarly, teachers could use it as an excuse to give up on certain pupils or focus their attention elsewhere. As effective educators, we must genuinely believe that all children have the potential to learn mathematics, focusing on depth of understanding rather than speed and focusing on the learning process rather than concentrating solely on outcomes. If we hold this belief, we will have patience with learners, look for different ways of demonstrating or explaining concepts and provide targeted support to pupils to ensure mastery of a concept before moving on. This approach will help 'children develop positive attitudes and interests in mathematics, look for patterns and relationships, spot connections, 'have a go', talk to adults and peers about what they notice and not be afraid to make mistakes' (DfE, 2021, p. 10). These behaviours are the ambitions of the EYFS framework, highlighting the importance of this aspect of teaching and learning mathematics alongside developing subject knowledge.

Teachers who are positive role models can and will positively influence the attitudes, values and behaviours of their pupils. These approaches will encourage resilience, inspire children to have a go and develop their beliefs in their own capabilities. This will also help overcome any feelings of maths anxiety as through exploration, play and discussions, in a safe and positive environment, children will not be afraid to make mistakes. Through this they will experience success in many different ways and in many different aspects of mathematics.

THE KNOWLEDGE QUARTET

Building on all these ideas, Rowland, Turner, Thwaites and Huckstep conducted an in-depth study into the knowledge of teachers of primary mathematics, from their starting points as trainees. They used their findings to create a framework that can support the development of essential subject knowledge for the teaching of mathematics and, as explained, this is one of the cornerstones upon which this book is based. Rowland et al. (2009) analysed a wide range of indicators of teacher knowledge and were able to classify them into 18 'codes' that they grouped under the headings shown in the table below. The 'codes' give us a definition of what each type of knowledge consists of. Beliefs also form a core part of foundational knowledge (Table 3.1).

Exploration of these ideas underpins the chapters on effective pedagogy in this book. It is also important to note that very similar ideas were highlighted in the Education Endowment Foundation's (EEF, 2020) recent summary of recommendations, following their meta-analysis of effective practice and subsequent report on 'Improving mathematics in the Early Years and Key Stage 1'.

Table 3.1 The codes of the Knowledge Quartet (Rowland et al., 2009, p. 29)

The codes of the Knowledge Quartet	
Foundation	Adheres to textbook Awareness of purpose Concentration on procedures Identifying errors Overt subject knowledge Theoretical underpinning Use of terminology
Transformation	Choice of examples Choice of representation Demonstration
Connection	Anticipation of complexity Decisions about sequencing Making connections between procedures Making connections between concepts Recognition of conceptual appropriateness
Contingency	Deviation from agenda Responding to children's ideas Use of opportunities

ACTIVITY

Reflect on how the EEF's (2020) five overarching recommendations (listed below) complement ideas discussed so far in this chapter.

1. Develop practitioners' understanding of how children learn mathematics
2. Dedicate time for children to learn mathematics and integrate mathematics throughout the day
3. Use manipulatives and representation to develop understanding
4. Ensure that teaching builds on what children already know
5. Use high-quality targeted support to help all children learn mathematics

Reflect on which of these are personal priorities for developing your practice.

BUILDING YOUR OWN MATHS KNOWLEDGE AND CONFIDENCE

As discussed in the previous section, subject knowledge for teaching mathematics consists of three key elements; subject-matter knowledge, curriculum knowledge and pedagogical content knowledge. A secure understanding of the relevant subject-matter knowledge is essential to underpin pedagogical practices. This book has a targeted focus on the Reception year, so this section explores key teaching and learning points relating to the expectations of the EYFS for mathematics by the end of the Reception year. The non-statutory guidance documents for the EYFS help give a clear overview of the learning trajectories that scaffold children's developing understanding of mathematics throughout the Early Years. The subsequent chapters in this book focus on key aspects of effective pedagogical content knowledge for teaching mathematics in the Early Years, drawing on the principles from Rowland et al.'s (2009) Knowledge Quartet.

The aspects of subject-matter knowledge discussed in this section are by no means an exhaustive list. We have tried to give the 'headlines' for key ideas in these areas to provide a fairly concise overview of relevant subject-matter knowledge. Each aspect can be explored in much more depth, and we have included recommendations for further reading at the end of the chapter.

The EYFS statutory framework (DfE, 2021, p. 10) states that:

> *Developing a strong grounding in number is essential so that all children develop the necessary building blocks to excel mathematically. Children should be able to count confidently, develop a deep understanding of the numbers to 10, the relationships between them and the patterns within those numbers. By providing frequent and varied opportunities to build and apply this understanding - such as using manipulatives, including small pebbles and tens frames for organising counting - children will develop a secure base of knowledge and vocabulary from which mastery of mathematics is built. In addition, it is important that the curriculum includes rich opportunities for children to develop their spatial reasoning skills across all areas of mathematics including shape, space and measures. It is important that children develop positive attitudes and interests in mathematics, look for patterns and relationships, spot connections, 'have a go', talk to adults and peers about what they notice and not be afraid to make mistakes.*

This overarching statement can be broken down into three areas for specific subject-matter knowledge: number, pattern and connections, and spatial reasoning.

ACTIVITY

Consider which elements of the mathematics statement relate to number, pattern and connection and spatial reasoning. Do any of these appear to be given more weighting?

While number may seem to be given more weighting, echoed by the fact that the summative outcomes of Early Learning Goals have a focus on Number and Numerical Patterns, it is essential to have a secure understanding of both spatial reasoning and pattern, recognising how they underpin children's developing understanding of number and other aspects of mathematics.

SPATIAL REASONING

'Spatial reasoning involves our interpretation of how things, including ourselves, relate to each other and our spatial environment and includes interpreting images and creating representations' (Early Childhood Maths Group [ECMG], 2022). The ECMG explains that spatial reasoning can be split into two key aspects (that while theatrically distinct, often overlap in practice). These are:

- Spatial relations: position, direction and routes, perspective-taking, transformations
- Objects and images: composing and decomposing shapes, transformations (including symmetry and tessellation)

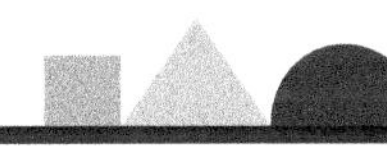

ACTIVITY

Jot down all the different ways you can think of that these aspects of spatial reasoning can be included in Early Years practice. Think inside and outside!

It is essential that developing spatial reasoning is incorporated into classroom practice. Through their research, Gilligan, Hodgkiss, Thomas and Farran (2019) explain there is a link between spatial skills and mathematical thinking from the age of three years, and they identify spatial skills as 'significant predictors of several mathematics outcomes.' Spatial reasoning skills underpin pattern work, which in turn underpins number work. In their daily routines and play children will naturally develop their spatial reasoning but will benefit from a wide range of opportunities to do this, both guided and independent. Through these opportunities, children benefit from being able to move themselves and objects around, exploring different viewpoints and perspectives. As children engage in these activities, look for opportunities to develop their use of maths-specific spatial vocabulary, in relation to both position and direction. It is important that while these two areas usually come hand-in-hand in everyday life, we create opportunities to focus specifically on positional vocabulary (in, on, under etc.) or directional vocabulary (up, down, forwards, backwards etc.). Words such as 'left' or 'right' can be particularly tricky as not only are they reliant on perspective, but they also have connotations for both position (on the left-hand side, to the right of) and direction (turn left, take three steps to the right). Identifying the 'trickier' words that have potential to cause confusion, either from reliance on perspective or dual uses, and focusing activities on these will be beneficial for developing the children's depth of understanding and confidence to use precise mathematical vocabulary to express ideas.

Opportunities for developing spatial reasoning are endless and include block play, den building, tangrams, jigsaws, construction, obstacle courses, PE lessons, using maps, hide and seek... the list goes on! Children will also benefit from opportunities to represent their spatial reasoning, for example drawing maps or creating plans for their construction designs (Williams, 2022). This will help develop their reasoning and justification skills whist further developing their understanding of different viewpoints and perspective. The ECMG (2022) gives practical suggestions for how to develop spatial reasoning in their 'Spatial Reasoning Toolkit', the link to which is in the suggested 'Further Reading/Resources' at the end of the chapter.

MEASURES

The EYFS statement for mathematics specifies children should 'develop their spatial reasoning skills across all areas of mathematics including shape, space and measures' (DfE, 2021, p. 10). While it may be clear how shape and space would be explored through the activities suggested above (and shape is explored in more detail in the pattern section), it is important to consider how understanding of measures develops spatial reasoning. Throughout history mathematical thinking has been created and developed to solve particular problems, many of which revolved around a need to measure. As such, there is an interesting argument that number should be taught through exploration of measure, rather than measure being taught as an application of number work... either way, there are lots of opportunities to develop connections and develop understanding of both skills.

Exploration of measure will initially focus on children identifying attributes to measure, for example how tall something is, how heavy it is or how much it can hold. As children naturally explore these ideas, it is important to model careful use of language. The word 'big' is ironically very am*big*uous! Developing specific vocabulary is important, while helping children identify word families in relation to different attributes they want to measure, for example that height, length, width etc. all relate to measuring length.

Early measurement follows a progression, which not only develops children's understanding of the purpose of measures but also of key measurement skills. This progression begins in the Early Years' exploration of measures and is formalised as children move into the National Curriculum expectations. Children begin measuring by direct comparison. The language of this is important too, modelling when to use –er or –est depending on whether two or more objects are being compared and identifying the occasions when it is appropriate to use more or most. Direct comparison also ensures children are introduced to key measurement skills such as needing to have the same starting place. This focus on measurement for comparison highlights to the children the need to compare objects and discuss different attributes. Through this their spatial reasoning will develop, as they decide whether objects (including themselves) will fit in a given space, how much something can hold before it overflows and how objects compare to each other.

Progressing from direct comparison children begin to use units (initially non-standard progressing to standard units) to measure objects in order to define their attributes. Here key measurement skills such as the starting and finishing points for measurement need to be considered and discussed, alongside not leaving gaps between the objects being used to conduct the measuring. Through exploring the use of non-standard measures, and potentially getting different measurements for the same objects, children reason about and appreciate the need for standard measures.

As children's understanding of measures develops into the use of units, it will become linked with number. Here children's understanding of comparison of number will become evident. Hewitt (2009, pp. 11–12) explains that the first step in the hierarchy of children learning about units for measures is about children 'saying number names and getting an ideas of relative size of numbers'. At this stage children will tell you something's really tall so it must be 'a million' tall or really short so only about '2 high'. From this starting point children then learn to give a unit name at the end of a number, then give an appropriate unit for the context, before finally using appropriately sized numbers for the units and contexts (ibid).

PATTERN

Many opportunities for developing spatial reasoning will lead to children exploring pattern and connections, both through guided and free play activities. As mentioned in the previous chapter, pattern is at the heart of mathematics and as humans we are innate pattern spotters. Su (2020, p. 53) explains that 'a seasoned math explorer begins to expect enchantment – to believe that patterns abound everywhere, waiting to be uncovered'. Exploration of pattern forms the basis of mathematical thinking and reasoning. When children are given the opportunity to explore and create patterns, realising what rules they follow while noticing any changes or irregularities, the structures for mathematical thought can be encouraged and developed.

In the Early Years, children are most likely to engage with repeating patterns (creating sequences of objects or images), spatial patterns (recognising shapes with specific properties or arranged in accordance with a rule) or growing patterns (equally spaced staircase patterns or growing tile patterns) (Borthwick et al., 2021). Understanding of these patterns can be developed through playful exploration of shape and many other stimuli, such as musical rhythms, using beads or trains, loose part play both inside and outside, and growth patterns in the narrative of story books. Once children are adept at spotting patterns and are encouraged to verbalise the rules for the patterns they find, these ideas can easily be applied to finding patterns in the number system, patterns in how numbers are composed and patterns in how numbers are used. Borthwick et al. (2021) explore the importance of pattern, its inclusive nature and offer practical activities for using pattern to develop creative thinking and mathematical reasoning in 'The Power of Pattern – Patterning in the Early Years', recommended in the 'Further Reading/Resources' at the end of the chapter.

SHAPE

When incorporating shapes, it is important to ensure that the examples used will help the children develop a thorough understanding of shape. It is also important to be aware of misconceptions children may have formed as they engage with shape on a daily basis. Often 3D shapes are referred to by 2D shape names (both in videos and by animated shape sorter toys for example). Shape toys often have curved edges or corners so children will incorporate this into their understanding of what a shape looks like. A key aspect of exploring shape in the Early Years will be to help children recognise these misconceptions, and develop understanding of relevant properties such as flat, straight, curved or pointy. Children also need to be introduced to a wide range of examples for each shape, including 'not quite' examples, so they develop a broad understanding of what a shape could look like (these ideas are discussed in more depth in Chapter 5).

This emphasis on shape exploration lays the foundations for understanding the properties of shapes in more depth as the children progress to Key Stage 1. The progression in the expectations is in keeping with the van Hiele Levels of Geometric Thinking. Husband-and-wife team, Pierre and Dina van Hiele, proposed that children move through a framework for developing geometric thinking. The focus on recognising shapes is in keeping with the first level of the model, visualisation.

Here children judge shapes by their appearance, focusing on them as a whole rather than distinguishing their specific properties, which is the second level, description. The next level is informal deduction, where children can deduce properties of shape, based on their other properties and recognise relationships between them. It is these first three levels that are most relevant to practice in Early Years and Key Stage 1. Van Hiele (1999) explains development through the levels requires specific teaching and instruction, focusing children's attention on the relevant properties and required reasoning skills, but advocates taking a playful approach to exploration and progression.

NUMBER

The Early Leaning Goals for mathematics (DfE, 2021, pp. 12–13) focus on number but, as discussed, are underpinned by spatial reasoning and pattern (Table 3.2).

Table 3.2 Mathematics early learning goals

Number ELG	**Numerical patterns ELG**
Children at the expected level of development will: • Have a deep understanding of number to 10, including the composition of each number; • Subitise (recognise quantities without counting) up to 5; • Automatically recall (without reference to rhymes, counting or other aids) number bonds up to 5 (including subtraction facts) and some number bonds to 10, including double facts.	Children at the expected level of development will: • Verbally count beyond 20, recognising the pattern of the counting system; • Compare quantities up to 10 in different contexts, recognising when one quantity is greater than, less than or the same as the other quantity; • Explore and represent patterns within numbers up to 10, including evens and odds, double facts and how quantities can be distributed equally.

The final section of this chapter explores key subject-matter knowledge that will help underpin effective teaching and learning in relation to these goals.

Number sense may be a term you are familiar with; it draws together many key areas of developing an initial understanding of number. While an exact definition of number sense is debated, at its heart, number sense involves an understanding of what numbers are, their magnitude, and the different ways they can be composed and decomposed. This information can then be used flexibly to compare numbers, explore their relationships and underpins understanding of early calculation and estimation (adapted from Parrish, 2014).

From this we can consider number sense to comprise three main aspects:

- Understanding number in terms of quantity
- Appreciating part-whole relationships
- Being able to compare numbers.

These three aspects can be related to the underpinning areas of the Early Learning Goals, as understanding number in terms of quantity is underpinned by understanding counting and cardinality whist appreciating part-whole relationships and being able to compare numbers is underpinned by developing subitising, composition and comparison.

COUNTING AND CARDINALITY

When teaching counting, it is very important to be clear about exactly what it is you intend to teach and what you want children to learn. Counting can be associated with many different aspects of early mathematics such as developing a sense of quantity, understanding order and place value. Counting also becomes associated with calculation as ideas such as 'one more or one less' and 'counting on or counting back' are introduced.

It can be trickier than we realise to teach counting, as it is something that most of us take for granted, something that we can do naturally and probably do not remember learning. As such, it is important to be able to identify what is at the heart of an error or misconception when children are at the initial stages of learning to count. The seminal work of Gelman and Gallistel (1978) identifies five principles that underpin learning to count. These principles are listed below and we explore their application for both assessment and developing children's understanding.

- The **one-to-one** principle: While children often learn to count in a sing-song way or an exercise in memory, this can lead to the one-to-one principle not being applied. Imagine a child singing along to a counting song, pointing randomly at objects while they count. Unless they have a secure understanding that for every number they say, they must point to one object, they are likely to point with the rhythm of the song or their recital of the numbers. Giving children opportunities to count while physically touching or moving objects can help develop their understanding of this key principle.
- The **stable-order** principle: Children will often learn to count through repetition, be it in in the form of songs, stories or rhymes. As they become more familiar with the different ways of counting, they will come to realise that the numbers are always in the same order. Mistakes in counting owing to this principle are often characterised by children being consistently one number out

when they are counting, due to missing a number in the sequence. For example, counting, 'one, two, three, four, five, seven, eight...' The child knows the rest of the sequence, so repetition and emphasis will need to be made of the missing number. A problem with the stable order principle may be a little trickier to spot if children are swapping two numbers around, for example, 'one, two, three, five, four, six...' Here the child will arrive at the correct final number (unless of course they are counting four or five objects) so mistakes may only be noticed through lots of opportunities to count with and listen to the child.

- The **cardinal** principle: To understand the cardinal principle, children need to understand the purpose of counting – to find the total number of items in a set. We might notice children not stopping counting when they have reached the last object in a set or stopping before counting all the objects. Helping children understand the purpose of counting, through daily activities and contexts, will help develop their understanding of this principle.
- The **abstract** principle: Children's initial experience of counting will be counting objects they can manipulate or pictures they can point to. The abstract principle is when children realise they can count things that they cannot see. We need to create opportunities for children to practise this, encouraging them to visualise what it is they are counting.
- The **order-irrelevance** principle: The key aim within this principle is for children to realise that the cardinality of a group does not change if the objects are counted in a different order or moved around within the group. This can be a tricky concept for children to understand and relies on a good understanding of the cardinal principle. Modelling counting objects in different ways, or having children count the same group of objects in different ways, will help develop understanding of this.

Another key thing to be aware of in this area is the tricky teen numbers. Once children do count beyond twenty, they can be encouraged to spot the 'tens then units' pattern in counting. However, while the teens do have this format when they are written, they are spoken giving the unit value before the tens. This can cause confusion for children when they need to write a teen number, for example, sixteen written as 61. While we are discussing the tricky teens, thirteen sounds a lot like thirty and fifteen a lot like fifty and they are not the only ones! Creating lots of opportunities to visualise numbers will be key to helping children understand the difference and the composition of the teen numbers.

SUBITISING

There are two aspects of subitising. The first is **perceptual subitising**. This refers to the natural ability most children have to recognise the number of objects in a small set without having to count them. Perceptual subitising can help children visualise numbers, including aspects such as their composition and cardinality, ideas which relate to developing number sense.

While perceptual subitising involves instant recognition of quantities, **conceptual subitising** can help develop children's understanding of addition and subtraction. Here, children will use clues in the layout or pattern of objects to spot smaller groups to combine in order to identify the overall quantity.

Both types of subitising can be developed in children through teaching and playing. Domino and dice games will automatically encourage recognition of standard dot patterns. Hidden object type games, where a small number of items are hidden and briefly revealed will encourage recognition of non-standard patterns for perceptual subitising and can be used more deliberately to encourage conceptual subitising.

COMPOSITION

Developing conceptual subsisting and developing an understanding of the composition of numbers will naturally go hand-in-hand. Careful choice of resources will help children make the transition from subsisting to a more structured exploration of the composition of numbers. Structured resources such as Numicon will enable children to spot different way of composing and decomposing a number (Figure 3.6).

For example, when examining the 'five' piece of Numicon, children can first count the holes to ensure their understanding of its cardinality. This focus also develops understanding of 'five' as being composed of five ones. Different ways 'five' could be composed can then be explored. Children may see a one with four underneath, or two on the left-hand side with three on the right-hand side. Perhaps some children

Figure 3.6

will spot that the four can be further composed as two twos, so five is made up of one, two and two. Number composition is not limited to findings pairs of numbers, which is later developed through exploration of number bonds.

The EYFS framework (DfE, 2021, p. 13) suggests children should be encouraged to explore first the numbers to five, developing their subitising of these numbers. This is then extended to the numbers to ten. As they explore these numbers, they should be encouraged to spot patterns between the numbers, for example that when using Numicon, the odd numbers will always have a one on top with an even number underneath. The exploration needs to be more than visual otherwise the fact that even numbers can be comprised as a one added to an odd number may be missed. Children can practically overlay other Numicon pieces onto the number they are exploring, trying to find patterns in the way the composition of the numbers develop and convincing themselves and others that they have found all the combinations. Here, encouragement of systematic working also encourages the mathematical behaviours of reasoning and justification. Exploration of composition should not be limited to structured resources as encouraging children to use counters or other objects to create groups within numbers enables children to discuss their ideas and explore a range of different arrangements (these ideas are explored further in Chapter 5: Can we feel it and see it?).

Exploration of the composition of numbers lays the foundations for understanding part-whole models for numbers and number bonds. When developing understanding of number bonds, children need to be encouraged to focus on pairs of numbers that make the given number. Again, encouraging pattern spotting, which leads to a systematic approach and justification, helps develop both confidence and early mathematical behaviours.

COMPARISON

Comparing numbers relies on a secure understanding of the cardinal principle alongside an understanding of the order and position of numbers. Comparing is a very natural activity for children, who are always interested in what's bigger, who's taller and most importantly who gets the largest share of sweets! To support their ability to compare numbers, children need to develop their understanding that the value of a number becomes greater as they count forward through the positive numbers. In time, children will develop a mental image of the number line in their head, but much use of visual number lines, finger counting and other resources will underpin this.

Comparing groups of objects will enable children to understand the principle of 'more than' and 'fewer than', especially when introduced in relatable contexts.

Applying these principles to counting makes links between early addition and subtraction as 'one more' and 'one less' relationships are introduced for counting and comparison.

When considering sets of objects for comparison, there are a couple of important examples to include. It is important to include examples where there are the same numbers of objects. This gives children an opportunity to express their understanding of equal quantities, an idea that will underpin much of later number and calculation work. It is also beneficial to include examples where there are fewer larger objects being compared to more smaller objects. Here children will learn that it is the overall quantity that needs to be compared, requiring children to draw on the cardinality of the group, rather than judging by how large the group looks. Similarly, offer opportunities to compare groups of objects that are well spaced out to ones that are closely grouped.

PROGRESSION INTO EARLY CALCULATION

While calculation is not a specific focus of the EYFS, an understanding of how this develops and is underpinned by the mathematics in the Early Years is beneficial. The most important thing to note is that for each of the four operations, there are different structures which underpin the calculations, depending on the context, and much of the early work on number sense underpins these. Understanding the composition of numbers will also help children appreciate the inverse relationships between addition and subtraction and multiplication and division, including doubling and halving.

In terms of *addition*, Haylock (2019) explains that initially children will use an **aggregation structure**. This explores the idea of *how many altogether* and in early addition this will focus on *counting all* to find the answer. This should be progressed to an **augmentation structure** which explores situations when a given quantity is increased by a given amount. In early addition this will usually involve a *counting on* structure to find the answer. In practice, it is beneficial to find scenarios when the first number is given, but not countable. For example, there are five cows already in the shed, two more go in, how many are now in the shed? This can then be worked through with a model of the shed with the unseen five cows inside, with two more being modelled going in to join them.

While both structures for addition are clearly underpinned by children's understanding of counting and cardinality, counting on is a more efficient structure for addition than counting all. Children then need to be encouraged to use their understanding of the composition of numbers and numbers bonds to further develop their flexibility and efficiency with addition. Using number bonds enables children to efficiently decompose numbers to solve addition calculations. For example, when asked to calculate $7 + 5$, a child can draw on the fact that five is composed of a two and a three and relate this to knowledge of number bonds to ten to first calculate $7 + 3 = 10$, then $10 + 2 = 12$. This progression through addition strategies needs to be taught carefully and specifically but ultimately will only be successful if children have a secure grounding in counting, cardinality and composition.

For *subtraction*, the **take away** structure has similar links to counting and cardinality as the augmentation (counting on) strategy for addition. For both, it is important to note a common misconception that can be noticed if the children are one out each time they give an answer. This occurs when the child uses the given starting number as the first number for counting on or back. For example, they may answer that $7 - 3 = 5$, counting back, 7, 6, 5. Number line work can help support conceptual understanding of these strategies, focusing on finding the starting point and then bouncing forward or backwards as appropriate. In turn children should be encouraged to apply their knowledge of the composition of numbers and number bonds to subtraction calculations in a similar way to that of addition. Another key structure for subtraction is that of **finding the difference**. This is underpinned by children's work on comparison of numbers and developing this to find the difference in the magnitude between the cardinality of the numbers.

Early work on the composition of number can also support children's later understanding of *multiplication* and *division* structures. If children are encouraged to spot patterns such as 4 being composed of 2 twos, 6 being composed of 3 twos and 8 being composed of 4 twos etc. both the additive nature of multiplication and the pattern in the structure of the even numbers can be explored. Doubling numbers is also an early introduction to multiplicative thinking and patterns such as the outcome of doubling numbers always being even can be identified and reasoned about.

Understanding the composition of numbers will also underpin understanding of the structures of division. **Sharing** is a very instinctive and everyday activity for children, so exploring the equal groups that can be created is a natural extension of decomposing numbers. Halving is a way of exploring this notion, focusing on having just two equal shares, or in fact two equal groups, within a number. Exploring how halving applies to odd and even numbers helps to further develop children's understanding of equality. **Grouping** is the second structure of division that children need to be aware of, considering how many groups of a number are within the original number, for example, 3 groups of two can be found in six. Children need to be introduced to examples and scenarios involving both structures for division, as whilst the sharing structure may be more intuitive, later formal work on division tends to rely on the grouping structure.

SUMMARY

Hopefully, while reading this chapter, you have taken the opportunity to reflect on your own views of mathematics and your relationship with the subject. It is important to remember that 'subject knowledge' in mathematics is more than just subject-matter knowledge and that an effective teacher of mathematics will understand the place of the mathematics they are teaching in the children's learning trajectory, alongside understanding how the structures of mathematics in the Early Years underpin later mathematical learning. We encourage you to take the time to develop any areas you feel unsure about in your subject-matter knowledge whilst also looking for opportunities to celebrate your own, and the children's, positive relationship with mathematics.

FURTHER READING/RESOURCES

Birth to 5 Matters: Non-statutory guidance for the early years foundation stage. https://birthto5matters.org.uk/

Borthwick, A., Gifford, S., & Thouless, H. (2021). *The power of pattern – Patterning in the early years.* ATM.

DfE (revised 2021a). *Development matters.* https://assets.publishing.service.gov.uk/government/uploads/system/uploads/attachment_data/file/988004/Development_Matters.pdf

Education Endowment Foundation. (2020). *Improving mathematics in the early years and key stage 1.* https://educationendowmentfoundation.org.uk/education-evidence/guidance-reports/early-maths

Gifford, S. (2018 revised 2021). *Subitising.* Nrich. https://nrich.maths.org/14004

Haylock, D., & Cockburn, A. (2017). *Understanding mathematics for young children* (5th ed.). London: SAGE.

NCETM Early Years. https://www.ncetm.org.uk/in-the-classroom/early-years/

REFERENCES

Anderson, R. K., Boaler, J., & Dieckmann, J. A. (2018). Achieving elusive teacher change through challenging myths about learning: A blended approach. *Education Sciences*, *8*(3), 98–131.

Askew, M., Brown, M., Rhodes, V., Wiliam, D., & Johnson, D. (1997). *Effective teachers of numeracy: Report of a study carried out for the teacher training agency*. London: King's College, University of London.

Boaler, J. (2014). *The mathematics of hope: Moving from performance to learning in mathematics classrooms*. youcubed: https://www.youcubed.org/resource/growth-mindset/

Boaler, J. (no date). *Positive classroom norms*. youcubed: https://www.youcubed.org/resource/growth-mindset/

Borthwick, A., Gifford, S., & Thouless, H. (2021). *The power of pattern – Patterning in the early years*. ATM.

DfE. (2021). *Statutory framework for the early years foundation stage*. https://assets.publishing.service.gov.uk/government/uploads/system/uploads/attachment_data/file/974907/EYFS_framework_-_March_2021.pdf

DfE. (revised 2021a). *Development matters*. https://assets.publishing.service.gov.uk/government/uploads/system/uploads/attachment_data/file/988004/Development_Matters.pdf

Early Childhood Maths Group. (2022). *Spatial reasoning toolkit*. https://earlymaths.org/spatial-reasoning/

Education Endowment Foundation. (2020). *Improving mathematics in the early years and key stage 1*. https://educationendowmentfoundation.org.uk/education-evidence/guidance-reports/early-maths

Gelman, R., & Gallistel, C. (1978). *The child's understanding of number*. Cambridge, MA: Harvard University Press.

Gillian, K. A., Hodgkiss, A., Thomas, M. S. C., & Farren, E. K. (2019). The developmental relations between spatial cognition and mathematic in primary school children. *Developmental Science, 22*(4), 19.

Haylock, D. (2019). *Mathematics explained for primary teachers* (6th ed.). London: SAGE Publications Ltd.

Hewitt, D. (2009). From before birth to beginning school. In J.Houssart & J.Mason (Eds.), *Listening counts: Listening to young learners of mathematics*. Stoke on Trent: Trentham Books Limited.

Parrish, S. (2014). *Number talks*. Sausalito, CA: Math Solutions.

Rowland, T., Turner, F., Thwaites, A., & Huckstep, P. (2009). *Developing primary mathematics teaching*. London: SAGE Publications Ltd.

Su, F. (2020). *Mathematics for human flourishing*. London: Yale University Press.

Van Hiele, P. (1999). Developing geometric thinking through activities that begin with play. *Teaching Children Mathematics*, *5*(6), 310–316. NCTM.

Watson, A. (2021). *Care, mathematics teaching* (Vol. 279, pp. 11–15). ATM.

Williams, H. (2022). *Playful mathematics for children 3 to 7*. London: SAGE Publications Ltd.

PART 2

KEY PRINCIPLES OF EFFECTIVE MATHEMATICAL PEDAGOGY

INTRODUCTION TO PART 2

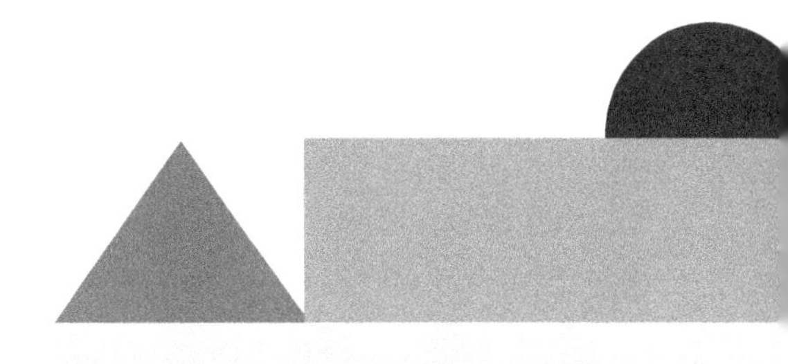

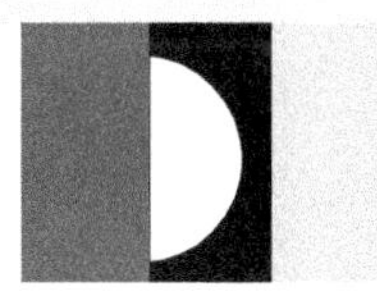

KEY PRINCIPLES OF EFFECTIVE MATHEMATICAL PEDAGOGY

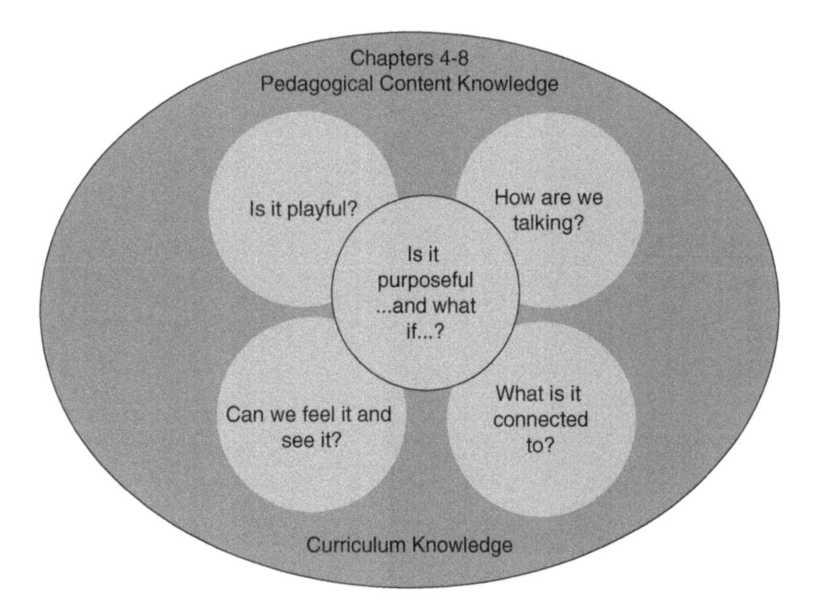

The following six chapters explore key principles of effective mathematical pedagogical content knowledge that will support your planning and provision for and teaching of mathematics. Inevitably, these pedagogies overlap, interconnect and underpin each other in a variety of ways, and separating them out in a linear form is in some ways a contrived activity for the format of a book! However, we hope to demonstrate how they can be viewed as offering essential elements of well-rounded mathematical teaching and learning in unique and complementary ways.

Throughout the chapters you will see that the principles of the EYFS: The Unique Child, Positive Relationships and Enabling Environments run as core considerations to ground the pedagogies for learning and development in the specific area of mathematics. The characteristics of effective learning; playing and exploring, active learning and creating and thinking critically are also embedded throughout.

Each of the five elements are applicable to planning for enhanced and continuous provision, and each chapter details the ways in which they contribute to high quality, and developmentally sensitive, guided learning. Examples, case studies and activities will be included to illustrate key points, but we acknowledge that there are countless high-quality resources available created by early mathematics educators and specialists that enhance and expand on these ideas. Signposting to relevant further reading and resources will be included throughout.

4

IS IT PLAYFUL?

CHAPTER OBJECTIVES

- Develop existing pedagogies of play in the Early Years, considering how these can have a targeted and supported maths focus
- Explore strategies for developing high-quality mathematical play

INTRODUCTION

> *Mathematics makes the mind its playground. Doing math properly is engaging in a kind of play: having fun with ideas that emerge as you explore patterns and cultivating wonder about how things work. Math is not about memorizing procedures or formulas, or at least that's not where you start. It's the same way in sports. In football, you wouldn't practice drills unless you wanted to play competitively, but you can start with an enjoyment of the game.*
>
> (Su, 2020, p. 50)

While play is recognised as a central part of an effective Early Years environment and as an integral part of children's learning, perhaps the association between maths and play, to many people, does not seem so natural. It may be that while much of the development in the Early Years is embedded in play, maths is seen as the outlier, the subject that is the focus of teacher-led teaching and practice. However, at its heart, mathematics is about spatial reasoning and pattern spotting, which both form key aspects of most play and playful exploration.

As stated in the Chapter 1, the Early Years Foundation Stage (EYFS) statutory framework's (DfE, 2021, p. 16) three characteristics of effective teaching and learning are:

- playing and exploring – children investigate and experience things, and 'have a go'
- active learning – children concentrate and keep on trying if they encounter difficulties, and enjoy achievements
- creating and thinking critically – children have and develop their own ideas, make links between ideas, and develop strategies for doing things

While 'playing and exploring' is defined here as a specific characteristic, through this chapter we will see how play also encompasses the characteristics of 'active learning' and 'creating and thinking critically'. Through embedding mathematics in play and play in mathematics, we are also able to encourage children to 'develop positive attitudes and interests in mathematics, look for patterns and relationships, spot connections, "have a go", talk to adults and peers about what they notice and not be afraid to make mistakes' (DfE, 2021, p. 10). As Pound and Lee (2022, p. 81) explain, 'children at play will try things out, refine them, come back to them, look at them from another angle, bring in other children to support the idea they are exploring, change roles and find reasons and solutions to problems that seem insurmountable. These are the same kids of engagement that we want our children to have in relation to mathematical enquiry and understanding.'

KEY IDEAS

ACTIVITY

What is play? Can you create a succinct definition for play? What are its key features?

Play is an innate part of us as humans – we want to play, whether that is babies exploring the world around them through exploration of their senses or grown-ups determined to finally win a game of monopoly! Play can be difficult to define as what is enjoyed as play can vary from person to person. Rather than defining play, Willams (2022, p. 7) highlights the behaviour of children as they engage with an activity as an indication of their playfulness, considering whether children are 'curious, motivated and creative', which she notes are also 'the factors that drive learning'. Creativity is an important aspect of play and, as Su (2020) explains, it is our imaginations that have a key role in developing play and sets our play apart from the playful antics observed throughout the animal kingdom. Tucker (2014, p. 3) notes that when children are being creative, they 'are captivated and curious [and] will be driven by this curiosity to achieve their goal.'

REFLECTION: TYPES OF PLAY

Su (2020, p. 49) notes there are different types of play: 'sports play, musical play, word play, puzzle play.' Jot down any other types of play you can think of. Do the types of play differ depending on the age of the participants? Are there some of these types of play you enjoy more than others? Why is this?

Kingdon and Palaiologou (2022) cite the following list of types of play that might be found within an Early Years environment (Figure 4.1).

ACTIVITY

Looking at the list of types of play, which can you immediately make mathematical connections to? Which might you need to think about in more depth to find links? Consider whether the links you are making are to spatial reasoning, pattern and connection or number. Can you find links for each of these aspects for the different types of play?

Su (2020, p. 49) draws our attention to the fact that facets of play 'run through nearly every human activity: dancing, dating, crafting, cooking, gardening an even "serious" activities like work and trade.' We consider connections that can be made to different aspects of everyday life and the EYFS framework in Chapter 7: What is it connected to? We would recommend keeping the key messages of playfulness in mind as you read that chapter and consider play-based possibilities when developing connections.

Types of play	Description	Examples
Symbolic play	When a child uses objects to symbolise for something else	A wooden spoon become a guitar or a big paper box becomes a castle where the child gets inside
Rough and tumble play	When children during their play become physical towards each other but with no intention to be violent	Children tickle each other
Socio dramatic play	The enactment of real-life situations or experiences	Children pretend they cook a meal or pretend They are fireworks
Social play	Children engage in play with rules of social interaction	Children have created a shop and they are buying and selling things using pieces of paper for money
Creative play	Children explore, try out new ideas and or making, changing things	A child takes a box of cereals and makes it into an armour
Communication play	Children engage in the use of words, songs, rhymes	Children pretend they talk on the phone or they present the news like the TV presenters
Dramatic play	Children dramatise events that were not directly participants	Children dramatise a popular show from the TV or a wedding
Locomotor play	Children play through movement	Children play musical chairs, chase, climbing
Deep play	Children engage in risky play	Walking on the top of a brick wall, balancing on a high beam, coming down the stairs jumping
Exploration play	Children engage in manipulative behaviours	Throwing, stacking bricks
Fantasy play	Children using imagination, they engage in make believe play	Children pretend they are astronauts travelling in space or they become giants climbing magic trees
Imaginative play	Children engage in play creating situations where the conventional rules do not apply	Running scared and shouting 'help' as they are 'chased' by a dragon
Mastery play	Children try to control the physical environment	Children dig a hole and carry water in it to make a lake
Object play	Children through their sense explore objects	Smelling flowers, touching fabrics and sense how they feel
Role play	Children take a role that is not associated with their normal domestic experiences	Children become taxi drivers, doctors, pilots
Recapitulative play	Children engage in play that allows them to explore ancestry, history, rituals, stories, rhymes	Children create a cave or an ancient temple

Figure 4.1

DEVELOPMENT OF PLAY

Tucker (2014, p. 1) emphases that 'play is what young children are about, it is what preoccupies them and it can be considered both a mode of behaviour and a state of mind.' It is important to note that as children grow and develop, play changes from individual play to communal play. Neaum (2019, p. 77) explains that children progress through stages of development in social play:

- **Solitary play**: This is an early stage of play. Children play alone and take no notice of other children who are around.
- **Parallel play**: A child plays side by side with other children, but without interacting. They may share space and possibly equipment, but their play remains independent of one another.
- **Associative play**: Children begin to play with other children. They make intermittent interactions and/or are involved in the same activity, but their play remains predominantly personal.
- **Co-operative play**: At this stage, children are able to play together cooperatively. They are able to adopt a role within a group and take account of others' needs and actions. Children understand and are able to keep to simple rules in their play.

In relation to these stages of development, it is relevant to us as educators that Howard, Jenwey, and Hill's (2006) research found children are more likely to perceive the later stages as play, rather than solitary activities. They also found that children associated the absence of the teacher with play. Kingdon and Palaiologou (2022) explain that for children to perceive an activity as play it should be enjoyable, it is likely to take place in a space rather than at a table and it will include peers rather than adults. This has implications for practice, as if children are to engage in co-operative play, it is essential to consider the characteristics of play and how we as adults can use these to help guide children's play to ensure it is as enjoyable (and purposeful) as possible, without necessarily being involved in the moment of play. Su (2020) explores the characteristics of play, explaining that for play to be successful it should be voluntary and meaningful; it will be underpinned by a structure or rules, but there is freedom to act within these rules. The freedom within the structure gives room for exploration, and this exploration can often lead to surprise and delight.

MATHEMATICS AND PLAY

ACTIVITY

We would like to invite you to play a quick game of connect four... If you are unfamiliar with the game, the aim is to get four of your colour discs in a row, either horizontally, vertically, or diagonally while stopping your opponent from doing so. Have a look at the images below and consider where you would put your next disc (you are red and have gone first). Try to explain why you have chosen that space. Were there alternative spaces you have discounted? (Figure 4.2)

(Continued)

(Continued)

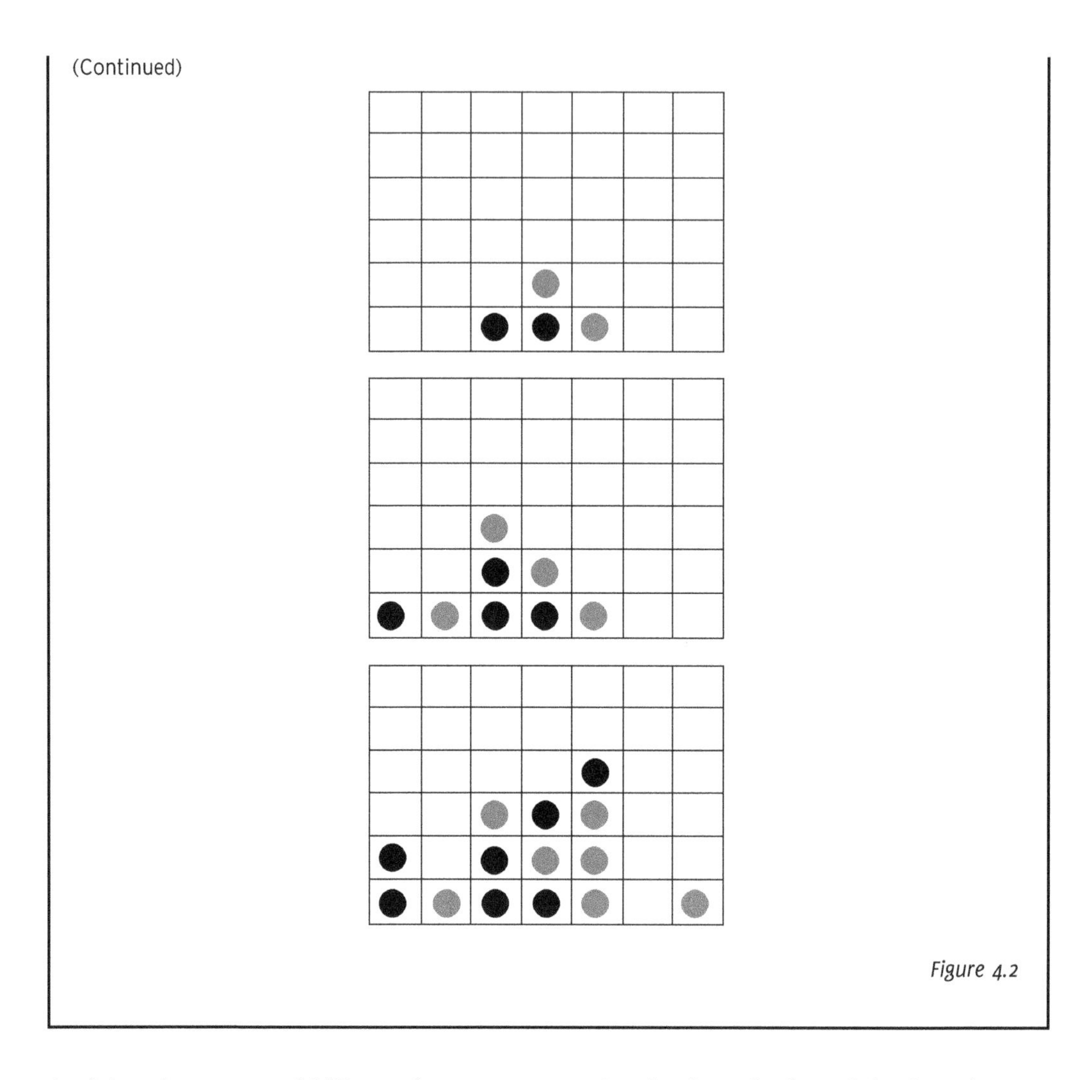

Figure 4.2

At this point, we would like to draw your attention back to the list of the foundations of mathematical thinking introduced in chapter two. It might be helpful to revisit your notes from the activity where you considered definitions for each of these terms.

The core foundations of mathematical thinking can be listed as:

- Exploring
- Questioning
- Working systematically
- Visualising
- Conjecturing
- Explaining

- Generalising
- Justifying
- Proving

(Nrich, 2020)

REFLECTION

How many of these thinking behaviours did you engage with when deciding where to go next in connect four?

The Education Endowment Foundation (EEF) (2020, p. 14) explain that 'games can be an engaging way to practise and extend skills. They can build on children's mathematical knowledge, generate repeated practice in a motivating context, and give children and practitioners an opportunity to discuss strategies and ideas.' Pound and Lee (2022) echo these ideas of games developing strategic thinking and emphasise that play and exploration are 'vital elements' (p. 48) of developing problem-solving strategies. They also highlight the enjoyment children get from creating their own games and the benefits of this as they learn about rule making and, through this, self-regulation.

ACTIVITY

Now consider other games that children play in your learning environments. Which of these thinking skills are they exhibiting? How could they be further encouraged to explore these through the rules and structures of their games?

Williams and Ollerton (2021, p. 5) believe that 'what is described as "play" in EYFS is often called "investigating" or "exploring" thereafter.' Whether we use the term 'playing', 'investigating' or 'exploring' we see how the same mathematical thinking behaviours can be encouraged. Tucker (2014) highlights that when children are being creative, they make links in their learning, refining and extending their thinking and evaluating their processes so as to be satisfied with the outcomes. Haylock and Cockburn (2017) also consider how problem-solving can sit within a play-based or specifically role play environment and how the elements of mathematical thinking can be enhanced and developed through this. Tucker (2014) explains that these creative behaviours can be enhanced and developed through the use of open-ended resources and questioning (explored further in Chapters 5 and 6), giving children time and space to explore and extend their enquiry, leaving resources out to return to later if necessary, and encouraging children to review their work, making links between maths and other experiences where appropriate. Similarly, Williams (Williams & Ollerton, 2021, p. 6) proposes that to create effective communities of mathematical learning classrooms should offer 'opportunities for children to get into the zone. Time to explore, to get involved, to play'.

UNIQUE CHILD

When considering play, it is important to remember that what one child considers to be play, another might not. So, if as Su (2020) highlights, play is going to be voluntary, we need to ensure children want to engage and become absorbed in the games or activities. Naturally, some children (just like adults) will be more interested in some games/activities and other children will be drawn to different games/activities. Having a range of good-quality games/activities, some that can be targeted to specific learning points when appropriate, will be key to engaging all children.

CASE STUDIES

Natalie was playing with the multilink and was making a staircase of numbers from one to ten, by making cubes into towers and lining them up next to each other. Unprompted, she then began taking the towers apart again, and restructuring the numbers, so they looked more like the Numicon shapes. At this point, she separated them out into odd and even numbers and made new staircase patterns (shown below) (Figure 4.3).

Figure 4.3

(Continued)

While she was doing this, the teacher had quietly gone and sat beside her, watching but not saying anything at this point. When Natalie had finished, she turned to her teacher and said, 'Look, I've made the numbers one to ten.' The teacher acknowledged this before asking, 'What's your favourite number? Have you made that?' Natalie replied, 'My favourite number is 100. I wonder if I can make it.' She then carefully started taking the towers apart again, to make a tower of ten. She then made another tower of ten and placed it alongside the first. 'Now I've got twelve' she said. 'Have you?' the teacher replied. 'I can see a ten [then starting to count on up the second tower] eleven, twelve...' Natalie interrupted at this point saying, 'No, I've got twenty! That means I'm going to need ten towers. I wonder if I'll have enough cubes?' The teacher left Natalie engrossed in her chosen mission but keeping an eye on her so she could check back in when Natalie had finished, celebrating her achievement with her and reaffirming that she had indeed made ten towers of ten.

Toby, a four-year-old in a Reception class, went up the teacher and quietly asked, 'Why is 9 an odd number?' Slightly surprised because the teacher was sure Toby had securely grasped this concept, they went and got out the Numicon. The teacher found a nine piece and invited Toby to look at the shape, noting that because of the 'sticking out' bit on top nine was an odd number. Toby replied, 'Yes but what if you lay it out as three threes, then it has a flat top.' This was not the response the teacher was expecting! They reminded Toby that when finding odd and even numbers, it needed to a 'two-s rectangle' as they called them. Toby smiled and nodded... but that's not where it ended! The teacher highlighted the fact that Toby had found a way to make a number into a square and wondered if there were any other numbers that could be laid out that way. Armed with some counters Toby went to explore different rectangles he could make from different numbers. When the teacher checked in with him a few minutes later Toby had explored a variety of numbers from 1 to 20, finding that 4, 9 and 16 could be made into squares. He also found that some numbers could only make 'one-s' rectangles. The teacher encouraged Toby to continue exploring other numbers which he did, discussing his findings as he went.

REFLECTION

What mathematical concepts were Natalie and Toby exploring through their play? What opportunities did they have to spot patterns and make connections? Which of the mathematical thinking behaviours were they demonstrating?

In both these case studies, the children are not engaging in traditional games or pre-planned activities. In both cases, the children were voluntarily entering into these opportunities and playing with mathematical ideas. Through this, they were also engaging with the mathematical thinking we discussed earlier. Both were visualising mathematical ideas, which led to their questioning and exploring, through which they began to work systematically. This sort of number play and exploration, underpinned by spatial reasoning, will ultimately help underpin Natalie and Toby's understanding of odd and even numbers, square numbers, area and particularly in Toby's case factors and prime numbers.

It is important to note that these examples may seem to contradict some of the previous discussions about children preferring co-operative play and play that is not taking place at a table. We wonder whether if asked Natalie and Toby would have identified these interactions as play? We would certainly classify them as playful. Both Natalie and Toby were enjoying themselves and showing engagement with all three characteristics of effective learning; playing and exploring, active learning, and creating and thinking critically. However, it is important to be mindful of individual responses to different stimulus and suggestions. Other children may not have wanted to continue with this exploration of their ideas in the same way. If they had been encouraged to do so less than voluntarily, then for them this would not be play!

REFLECTION

In his 2015 Ted^{x} talk '5 ways to share maths with kids' Dan Finkel explains, 'Einstein called play the highest form of research. Play gives the gift of ownership.' Consider how the above case studies exemplify this idea.

POSITIVE RELATIONSHIPS

As we consider positive relationship within the context of play, it is important to note that children and adult's perceptions of play may differ significantly, and that play is often considered from an adult perspective when considering curriculum opportunities (Kingdon & Palaiologou, 2022). It has already been noted that children tend to view play as situations that involve other children, rather than adults. Howard et al. (2006) highlight the need for children to accept adults as co-operative partners in play from an early age, so as to ensure educators can enrich and extend learning opportunities. Kingdon and Palaiologou (2022, p. 49) explain, 'adults need to ensure their participation is supportive, values children as equal play partners and does not dominate the play so that it becomes "work" rather than "play"'. So, while there is an argument that 'teachable moments need to be woven in child-initiated play' (DfE, 2021a), there is clearly a need to do this sensitively and in a way that does not cause the children to disengage from the play. There may also be times when it is more important to remain in the moment of play with the children, making a note of the opportunity for mathematics learning, but not acting on it at the time. Instead, it can be returned to as a stimulus or context for a specific learning opportunity at a later date.

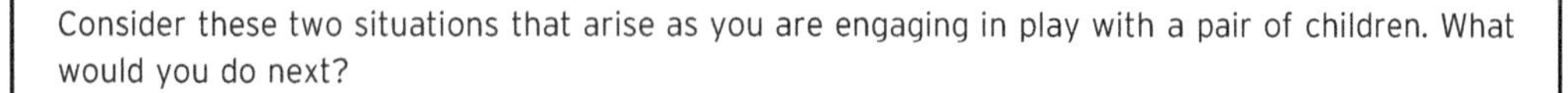

ACTIVITY

Consider these two situations that arise as you are engaging in play with a pair of children. What would you do next?

1. You are about to start a game of snakes and ladders with the children. The rules say you need to roll a six to start. One child says, 'but it's always harder to roll a six than any of the other numbers.'
2. The class photo has just taken place, and the children are lining up the toys to have their picture taken. The children are discussing the various heights of the toys as you work with them setting up the picture, but the comparisons of height are not being made mathematically...

The first situation could just lead to a quick opportunity for counting, noting the numbers one to six and having a discussion about why it seems harder to roll a six. Through playing games such as snakes and ladders, Haylock and Cockburn (2017) explain that children make connections between the number symbols on the dice, the name of the number and moving their counter forward appropriately. Through the underpinning grid structure and consecutive numbering, skills such as counting on can be developed (EEF, 2020) alongside developing children's broader number sense. Having quick but meaningful conversations as and when they arise (such as commiserating the bad luck of having to go down the longest snake or discussing whether you must roll an exact number to finish) can further enhance these benefits. These conversations can be casually integrated into the play and be as in depth or passing as you judge appropriate for the interests of the children involved.

The second scenario may create more debate in your mind, as there will be a number of ways you could proceed. There is also no right or wrong here, but ideally the children will take the lead in the direction that the play goes. You may engage with the play and through not interfering the children may realise that once all the toys are lined up their measuring system has been wonky, in which case they may start to naturally re-evaluate and ask questions. Here you may then want to offer prompts or suggestions to guide the children's thinking. Alternatively, once the toys are lined up it may be you who prompts the notion that actually 'nellephant' cannot be seen behind 'raffe'. Alternatively, you may choose not to say anything at all and just engage with the play, seeing where it leads and privately noting to yourself that it would be beneficial to plan some guided learning opportunities to explore measure and measurement skills. Again, knowing your children will inform whether those guided learning opportunities reference this activity and makes it the context for learning or not, as that would please some children but embarrass others – your positive relationships with the children will enable you to make that decision.

The EEF (2020, p. 17) highlight that 'through observing children's play, practitioners will identify "teachable" moments in which they can join the play to add to the discussion, reinforce mathematical vocabulary, and encourage problem-solving.' They suggest that to do this effectively, careful consideration of mathematical concepts, appropriate vocabulary and possible discussion points will be beneficial. As you read Chapter 6: How are we talking? consider how the key messages can be applied to these opportunities for engagement with play.

ENABLING ENVIRONMENTS

In our exploration of enabling environments for play, we consider opportunities for guided learning (specific teaching opportunities and guided play interventions) and enhanced and continuous provision (free play). Williams (2021) emphasises that for quality maths learning and provision, there needs to be a balance between high-quality maths teaching and well-considered opportunities for free play. Through establishing this balance, the status of both elements are increased. Through purposeful free-play activities children appreciate the need for maths so they will be more willing to engage in the taught elements; in turn the quality of maths in free play also increases (Clements & Sarama, 2021). Skene et al. (2022) define guided play 'as a "middle-ground" between free play and direct instruction' and have found it to have a positive effect on children's early maths and related skills.

GUIDED LEARNING

When considering specific teaching opportunities, it is important to acknowledge that maths is a subject where progress is built on conceptual understanding of a concept and having opportunities to practise the skills and ideas being learnt. While the statutory framework, does suggest potentially engaging ways for some of this practice ('such as using manipulatives, including small pebbles and tens frames for organising counting' [DfE, 2021, p. 10]) the idea of practice can still seem at odds to a playful environment. Williams (2021) explains the 'adult-initiated interactions with groups of children, small and large, need not be "telling shops", but instead be playful and truly interactive, taking children's ideas onboard.' As such, playful practice can be encouraged during specific teaching opportunities and guided play interventions as well and through the follow-up activities and the free-play provision in the learning environment.

Specific teaching opportunities may take place with the whole class or with a group of children and should have a specific learning goal in mind. However, Williams (2022, p. 9) notes that in mathematics teaching 'must allow space for children's sense-making as well as their own ideas'. She highlights the fact that prepared questions should not come too fast or too soon, allowing children time to think, talk and play with ideas. Skene et al. (2022) identify three key factors in effective guided play; the adult providing the activity needs to have a clear learning goal, the activity should allow for some child-led aspects of choice in the play and 'the adult should be flexible in their use of guidance techniques (e.g. by using open-ended questions, hints, prompts, modelling) to ensure sensitivity to the child's interests and needs'. Considering these definitions there will be many times when specific teaching opportunities could be synonymous with guided play interventions.

ACTIVITY

Choose one of the Early Years Number activities from the Nrich collection:https://nrich.maths.org/13372

Consider how the activity promotes specific teaching and practice and/or a guided play opportunity through a playful context for the concept being taught. How could these ideas also be embedded into free-play activities to support and consolidate the learning?

Some of learning benefits of games have already been considered in the positive relationships section. Williams (2022) ascertains that the simpler the game and the more familiar the participants are with it, then the more opportunities there are to develop mathematical thinking. She proposes a simple reasoning scaffold of '*if...then...because*' (p. 35). Referring back to the earlier snakes and ladders example and elaborating on it slightly, *if* we have decided that you don't need to roll an exact number to win, *then* Sam will win, *because* she is only one away from the finish square. This simple scaffold can be built upon as appropriate to develop the wider mathematical thinking behaviours of exploring, questioning, working systematically, visualising, conjecturing, explaining, generalising, justifying and proving.

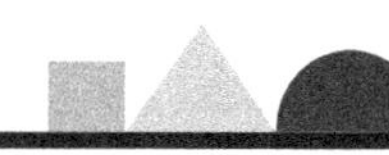

REFLECTION

Consider how this simple reasoning structure could be embedded into other children's games you are familiar with. How could the mathematical thinking be further developed if appropriate?

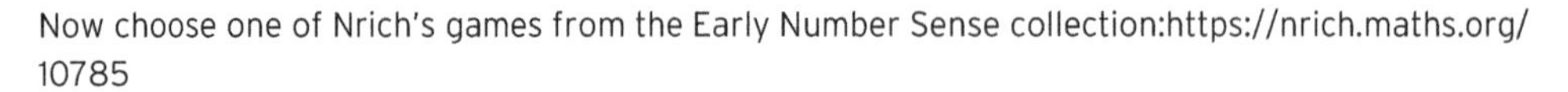

ACTIVITY

Now choose one of Nrich's games from the Early Number Sense collection:https://nrich.maths.org/10785

Consider what intended learning the game promotes and how you could use it for playful practice alongside encouraging mathematical thinking.

Chapter 5: Can we feel it and see it? promotes ways in which children can visualise mathematics, and this understanding of effective resourcing will be helpful to consider when planning for guided learning opportunities.

ENHANCED AND CONTINUOUS PROVISION

Much of the enhanced and continuous provision in a Reception classroom will naturally be opportunities for play. Pound and Lee (2022) suggest that play and exploration may look like 'messing about' but through this children have the opportunity of 'examining the limits between reality and non-reality, taking risks without serious consequences' (p. 48). It is important to consider how mathematical links and opportunities can be effectively promoted and explored. In keeping with the ideas discussed already in this chapter, the guidance in Development Matters' (DfE, 2021, p. 10) exploration of pedagogy suggests, 'Practitioners carefully organise enabling environments for high-quality play. Sometimes, they make time and space available for children to invent their own play. Sometimes, they join in to sensitively support and extend children's learning.'

When preparing the learning environment for enhanced and continuous provision, it is important to consider the mathematical potential the opportunities have. Reflect on whether the opportunities focus on spatial reasoning, pattern and connection, number, or a combination of these elements. When planning, be mindful of how these opportunities may lead to teachable moments or possible prompts for children to explore the provision in a slightly different way.

CASE STUDY

Bethany and Sophie were busy setting up a restaurant in the role play area. This was not the first time they had played restaurants and the teacher had noted their play and carefully considered how they could enhance the mathematical provision. There was a board and chalk available which Bethany and Sophie had used to create a menu (Figure 4.4). There was also a box of multilink

(Continued)

available, which was used as money, which the teacher had carefully prepared into premade columns of ten, five in one colour, five in another.

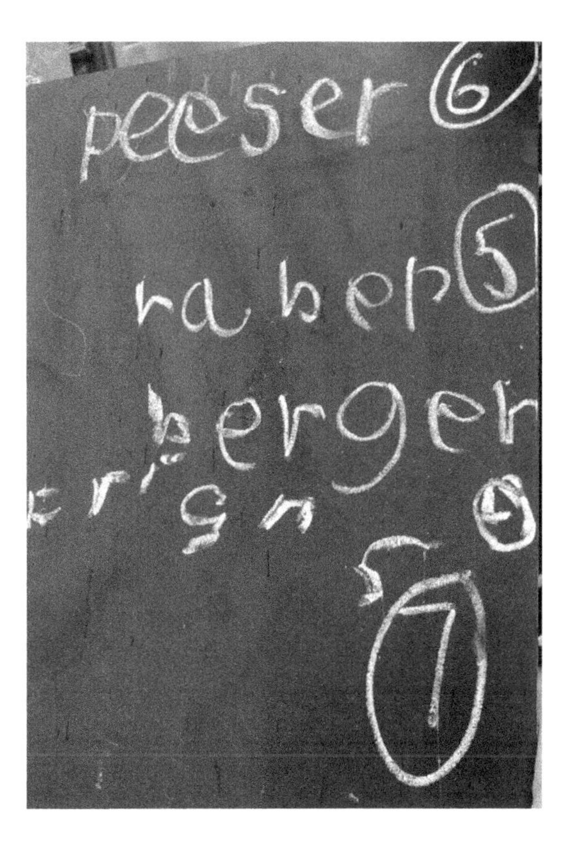

Figure 4.4

During the course of their play, a visitor from another class came in and was quickly invited to dine at the restaurant. Bethany explained that they could come to the restaurant and have anything they wanted. The guest looked at the menu and asked for a hamburger (haber) but explained to Bethany that they did not have any money to pay. At this point, Bethany and Sophie were very quick to put their visitors' mind at rest! 'That's ok' said Sophie, and pulled over the box of multilink, 'You just use these'. Bethany went on to say, 'The burger is 5, so you just give us half [at which point she snapped the multilink tower]. Here, you have these and we'll keep these.'

A little later, Jonah joined Bethany and Sophie. He asked for a pizza (peeser). Sophie helpfully gave him a tower of multilink, which he promptly gave back in payment. Unphased by this Sophie snapped six off and gave four back to Jonah. 'Here you go,' she said, 'I've got six, so you get four back.'

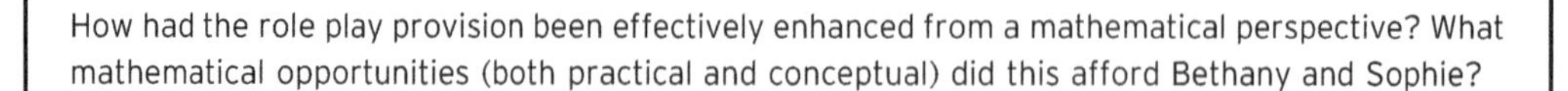

REFLECTION

How had the role play provision been effectively enhanced from a mathematical perspective? What mathematical opportunities (both practical and conceptual) did this afford Bethany and Sophie?

Haylock and Cockburn (2017) identify how role play environments can support problem-solving in a purposeful and child-led environment. Williams highlights (2022) an additional benefit that role play allows children to make and correct mistakes in a safe environment. This is important as children learn to 'have a go' and 'not be afraid to make mistakes' in their early mathematical explorations. Gifford (2006) does caution that mathematics in role play can become superficial, so it is important to consider how to make role play opportunities as mathematically purposeful as possible. Williams (2022) explores the benefits of providing children ways and means of recording their maths and mathematical thinking as they are engaging with it. This representation can have several benefits as children can explore designs in advance of creation, have opportunities to practise representation of mathematical stories or elements of play and enable children to show their reasoning as they solve problems within play environments.

REFLECTION

Consider how representation could be further encouraged in the restaurant role play case study. What mathematical learning might this support?

While some opportunities for games and play (including role play) will create overt opportunities for using number, many will offer opportunities for developing spatial reasoning. Williams (2018) explains how spatial reasoning develops from static to dynamic and incorporates the following elements:

- **understanding relationships** – how things fit together, how moving parts work
- **language** – hearing, describing, directing; position, direction
- **spatial memory** – where things are
- **sense of direction** – finding your way back
- **spatial representations** – creating mental images, composing and deconstructing; perspective and movement; understanding models, maps and diagrams.

ACTIVITY

- Consider how a treasure hunt could enable children to playfully and purposefully develop some of these elements.
- How could block play be used?
- What other playful activities could you provide in your enhanced or continuous provision which would allow children to explore these elements of spatial reasoning?

SUMMARY

Play is an integral part of Early Years practice. Play is also an integral part of understanding and exploring mathematics. Children naturally engage with mathematics in their play, and their mathematical thinking can be enhanced by well-timed and carefully considered adult preparation and/or participation. We began this chapter with a quote from Fransis Su as he explains how play is an essential part of maths for human flourishing. It seems only right to conclude with another:

> *Play is fundamental to who we are as human beings, and the desire for play can entice everyone to do, and enjoy, mathematics.*
>
> (Su, 2020, p. 64)

FURTHER READING/RESOURCES

Education Endowment Foundation. (2020). *Improving Mathematics in the Early Years and Key Stage 1.* https://educationendowmentfoundation.org.uk/education-evidence/guidance-reports/early-maths

Finkel, D. (2015). *5 ways to share math with kids.* TedxRainier. https://www.ted.com/talks/dan_finkel_5_ways_to_share_math_with_kids?language=en

Nrich. *Early number sense.* https://nrich.maths.org/10785

Nrich. *Early years activities.* https://nrich.maths.org/13371

Su, F. (2020). *Mathematics for human flourishing.* Yale University Press – Chapter 4: Play.

Tucker, K. (2014). *Mathematics through play in the early years* (3rd ed.). London: SAGE Publications Ltd.

Williams, H. (2022). *Playful mathematics for children 3 to 7*. London: SAGE Publications Ltd.

REFERENCES

Clements, D., & Sarama, J. (2021). *Learning and teaching early math: The learning trajectory approach*. (3rd ed.). New York: Routledge.

DfE. (2021). *Statutory framework for the early years foundation stage*. https://assets.publishing.service.gov.uk/government/uploads/system/uploads/attachment_data/file/974907/EYFS_framework_-_March_2021.pdf

DfE. (2021a). https://help-for-early-years-providers.education.gov.uk/mathematics/numbers

Education Endowment Foundation. (2020). *Improving Mathematics in the Early Years and Key Stage 1*. https://educationendowmentfoundation.org.uk/education-evidence/guidance-reports/early-maths

Finkel, D. (2015). *5 ways to share math with kids*. TedxRainier. https://www.ted.com/talks/dan_finkel_5_ways_to_share_math_with_kids?language=en

Gifford, S. (2006). *Teaching mathematics 3-5: Developing and learning in the foundation stage*. Maidenhead: Oxford University Press.

Haylock, D., & Cockburn, A. (2017). *Understanding mathematics for young children* (5th ed.). London: SAGE.

Howard, J., Jenway, V., & Hill, C. (2006). Children's categorisation of play and learning based on social context. *Early Childhood Development and Care*. *176*(3 & 4), 379–393.

Kingdon, Z., & Palaiologou, I. (2022). What matters in early childhood? In C. Carden (Ed.), *Primary teaching* (2nd ed.). London: SAGE Learning Matters.

Neaum, S. (2019). *Child development for early years students and practitioners* (4th ed.). London: SAGE Publications, Ltd.

Nrich. (2020). *Thinking mathematically*. https://nrich.maths.org/mathematically

Pound, L., & Lee, T. (2022). *Teaching mathematics creatively* (3rd ed.). London: Routledge.

Skene, K., O'Farrelly, C. M., Byrne, E. M., Kirby, N., Stevens, E. C., & Ramchandani, P. G. (2022). *Can guidance during play enhance children's learning and development in educational contexts? A systematic review and meta-analysis*. Child Development. https://doi.org/10.1111/cdev.13730

Su, F. (2020). *Mathematics for human flourishing*. London: Yale University Press.

Tucker, K. (2014). *Mathematics through play in the early years* (3rd ed.). London: SAGE Publications Ltd.

Williams, H. (2018). *Mathematics in the early years: What matters?* Impact: Chartered College. https://my.chartered.college/impact_article/mathematics-in-the-early-years-what-matters/

Williams, H. (2021). *Exploratory math and dedicated maths sessions. How both are important*. Ponderings on Maths Education. https://info125328.wixsite.com/website/post/exploratory-maths-and-dedicated-maths-sessions-how-both-are-important

Williams, H. (2022). *Playful mathematics for children 3 to 7*. London: SAGE Publications Ltd.

Williams, H., & Ollerton, M. (2021). *Revisualising: A vision for mathematics education, MT*. Vol. *279*, pp. 5–10, ATM.

5

CAN WE FEEL IT AND SEE IT?

CHAPTER OBJECTIVES

- Explore key theories connected to the importance of concrete, pictorial and abstract representations in mathematical learning
- Consider the ways in which mathematical concepts can be represented to show and develop mathematical thinking and understanding

INTRODUCTION

Of all the elements of pedagogical content knowledge that are considered essential for developing mathematical learning, that of 'representing the maths' is possibly the most well documented currently in terms of the resources and training that are available for educators. As Aubrey (1997) states, '...all mathematics concerns the representation of ideas to allow the manipulation of information or data' (p. 45). The 'Mastering Number' programme provided by the NCETM for Reception and Key Stage 1 teachers has this at its core, there are countless websites and textbooks available to provide activity ideas that utilise a wide variety of 'representations', and specific resources fall in and out of favour depending on the edu-fashion of the time. Much of these support materials reflect a curriculum preoccupation with learning number facts and becoming fluent, while implicitly relying on the development of spatial reasoning and an appreciation for pattern as crucial foundations for this. We will also consider how spatial reasoning forms a basis for geometric, measurement and statistical knowledge and understanding, and how representations of these can be incorporated into high-quality Early Years practice.

KEY IDEAS

Bruner's (1966) modes of representational thought are at the root of the theoretical developments relating to learning and meaning. He posited that learners need experience at three levels of thought – the enactive, the iconic, and the symbolic – in order to construct understanding of new material. Application of this to mathematical learning and development has been interpreted and re-interpreted over time. Lesh, Post and Behr provide a model for translations between modes of representation (1987, in Aubrey, 1997, p. 46) that incorporates the enactive through manipulative aids, the iconic in the form of pictures, the symbolic in terms of spoken and written symbols and builds on these with the addition of contexts to add meaning in the form of real-world situations. Crucially this model accentuates the need for connections between the elements and acknowledges that each can serve both a personal and social purpose.

Similarly, Liebeck (1990, p. 16) summarised how mathematical understanding is built up through making a network of connections between symbols, language, pictures and concrete experiences. She coined the acronym ELPS: E – *experience* with physical objects, L – spoken *language* that describes that experience, P – *pictures* that represent the experience, S – written *symbols* that generalise the experience. All of these models of learning have the idea that a child's perception and understanding of the (mathematical) world are fundamentally linked to structures of and connections between representations (Aubrey, 1997).

For all learners of mathematics, physical interaction with the environment, using our senses to immerse ourselves in ideas and processes, is key; '...our ideas are shaped by our bodily experiences – not in any simpleminded one-to-one way but indirectly, through the grounding of our entire conceptual system in everyday life' (Lakoff & Nunez, 2000, p. xiv). *Feeling* and *seeing* situations, objects, pictures, models and the effect of our interactions with them is therefore crucial and should become embedded in all mathematical environments. The physical resources provided could take the form of:

a) 'real' examples of the subject of mathematical problems, e.g. items of food, toys, people, clothes etc.,

b) 'loose parts' that make up sets of individual unit objects that can either be literal or figurative representations of the mathematical problem being thought about, e.g. counters, shells/pebbles, beads, multilink cubes, chain links etc., or

c) resources that have an inherent mathematical structure and draw attention to specific mathematical patterns, structures and relationships, e.g. Numicon, Cuisenaire rods, pattern blocks, rekenreks, Dienes blocks etc.

Of course, these are not mutually exclusive categories; 'real' examples and 'loose parts' can be used in ways that draw attention to mathematical patterns, structures and relationships, and examples from category 'c' can be used in ways that do not draw attention to their inherent mathematical attributes (although, depending on the context, this could be seen as a missed opportunity). We also cannot ignore perhaps the most literal embodiment of number and counting available to a large majority of children – their fingers! It could be argued that this fully portable and ever accessible mathematical resource fits all three of the above categories. This will be explored in more detail in the rest of this chapter, but the benefits of encouraging and supporting the use of fingers as manipulatives are increasingly well understood (Sarama & Clements, 2009).

UNIQUE CHILD

In order to meet the needs of each unique child, the provision of developmentally appropriate resources/manipulatives (alongside the development of high-quality dialogic talk which is covered in depth in Chapter 6) is key (Gardner & Jones, 2016). Interaction with and use of different representations of mathematical ideas touches on many complexities around the construction of mathematical knowledge for individual learners. These can be classified as relating to concepts, procedures, autonomy and progression.

CONCEPTS AND PROCEDURES

In Chapter 3, we touched on the integral idea of 'number sense' and how this is inseparable from an understanding of spatial reasoning and a strong awareness of pattern. In order that each child can develop the conceptual and procedural knowledge associated with a secure sense of number, they will need to have access to a wide variety of representations. Conceptual knowledge is defined as the 'relatedness' of ideas and facts that are rooted in general mathematical principles such as magnitude, equivalence, parts and wholes, while procedural knowledge refers to mathematical processes needed to solve calculations or problems. You will also see these two knowledges characterised throughout mathematics education as relational/instrumental knowledge, and a useful metaphor might be to consider the development of a mathematical map, versus a set of linear directions, in order to help learners 'find their way' (Skemp, 2006). Simply put, we can think of them as the 'why' and the 'how' of mathematical learning, although, of course, sometimes they overlap, for example when we might look for similarities and differences in methods for calculating or develop a conceptual understanding of amount thorough the procedural application of operations.

CASE STUDY

Children in Reception were asked to complete a home learning task to explore 'the three-ness of three'. Have a look at Artan's work shown below. What different examples of 'three-ness' can you identify? How would you assess Artan's conceptual understanding of 'three'? (Figure 5.1)

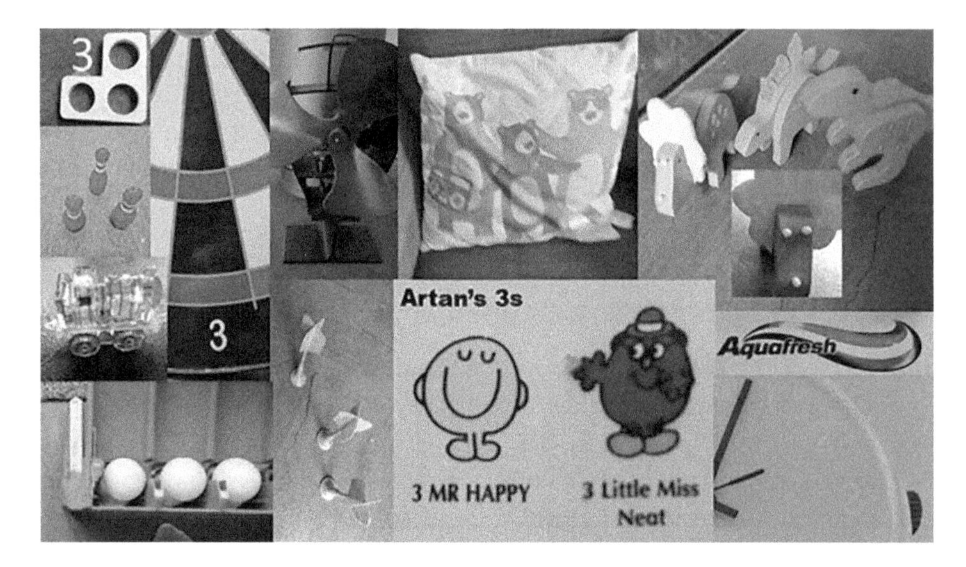

Figure 5.1

We see Artan has recognised the structure of 'three' when looking at the number of darts, dinosaurs, balls, bears etc. He also uses a mathematical representation through the inclusion of the Numicon piece. We also see a potential element of subitising as he identifies the three stripes in the toothpaste logo. Artan also recognises the digit three, as shown on the train, the dart board and the book characters. He also shows an awareness of counting to three, given the inclusion of the numbers one and two on the clock picture.

Developing early procedural knowledge is largely concerned with the core concepts of ordering, positioning and amount (Woodham & Pennant, 2018). Many of the manipulatives listed above will support the development of these ideas and potential resources can be expanded to include more iconic/visual/pictorial representations too. For example, number tracks or tiles (that include both pictorial and symbolic representations of amounts), number lines, dice, domino and board games and tens frames. Any matching or sorting activities are likely to support the development of connections between representations, and therefore deepen mathematical understanding.

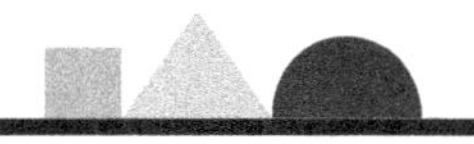

ACTIVITY

How could you support Artan to develop his conceptual and procedural knowledge in relation to the 'three-ness of three'? How could you utilise more representations to extend his ideas of what can be done with 'three'? Could you encourage him to investigate moving up and down a number track using 'three'? Or look at what happens when you have more than one group of three?

AUTONOMY

The use of and interaction with a range of representations of mathematical ideas is both a personal and social experience. They offer learners opportunities to construct and secure their individual understanding, they provide them with the means to communicate their thinking when linguistic or symbolic representations are insufficient or beyond their current capability, and they give us all something to talk *about* (Aubrey, 1997). Crucially, they are to be interacted with rather than provided as passive illustrations (Askew, 2018) and here there is the potential for each child to increase their autonomy in which representations they choose and how they use them. Choice is therefore a core component of effective practice and the provision of a wide range of manipulatives and images as part of continuous provision goes some way to cater for this. However, there are also occasions when we might want to enhance the provision in order to meet a specific need or advance mathematical thinking by leading children to the use of a resource that demonstrates a particular mathematical structure, hence developing a 'curriculum driven by the interests of the children but framed by the expertise of the teacher' (Gardner & Jones, 2016, p. 615).

CASE STUDY

Harry counts very confidently and favours the shells and buttons from his classes 'loose parts' to show this. However, he is reliant on counting on as a form of addition and his knowledge of the cardinality and composition of numbers from 5 to 10 is not secure. His Reception teacher begins to play alongside him and counts out five multilink cubes, organising them into a tens frame, one in each 'box'.

T: (counts the 5 cubes) I've made 5, how many more do I need to make 10?

H: (counts the empty boxes) You need 5 more.

T: Oh yes, I can see that there's a line of empty boxes that matches my 5 cubes. So, I can see that 5 and 5 is 10. I'm going to join my five cubes together.

(Continued)

(Continued)

Harry starts to play with the cubes and clicks two together saying 'I've made 2!'

T: So you have! Can you put that next to my five? What do you notice? I wonder if we can make another stick to put with the two that would make these the same length?

H: We need three more...

PROGRESSION

One of the most prevalent ideas in mathematics teaching, which forms a core part of the NCETM's mastery approach, is that children move from concrete to pictorial, to abstract representations when developing their mathematical understanding. Increasing awareness from the field of cognitive science lends weight to this argument, with many sources sharing the view that each child needs to gradually transition through these representations, progressing from simple, uniform manipulatives to those that are more complex and varied in a process called 'concreteness fading' (Deans for Impact, 2019). Gardner and Jones (2016) also discuss the need for each child to have access to developmentally appropriate materials and resources in order to scaffold their learning, and Clements and Sarama (2018) state that children need to move away from (solely) using manipulatives when they are able as they develop more sophisticated and mathematical representations.

However, while these views undoubtedly are of value and ought to be engaged with by all educators, there are some nuances and complexities in their application to individual children that need to be considered. First, there is an inherent assumption that it is possible to separate the three representations from each other. While it is possible to see how this might be true for the symbolic written form (digits, operation symbols etc.) and that some pictorial representations may be just that (e.g. dot patterns), it is often the case that concrete resources inherently contain iconic representations of mathematical concepts such as amount, magnitude and part-whole relationships. Similarly, some visual representations will have an element of 'manipulative' about them when interacted with on digital devices or interactive whiteboards. Second, there is a case to be made for learners to use concrete or visual representations to prove or disprove their abstract knowledge, such as when a conjecture, like 'odd numbers can't be halved', has been made. Third, it is difficult to categorise manipulatives into 'simple' or 'complex' in and of themselves, rather it is the ways in which they are used that can show simplicity or complexity of thought. Lastly, the assessment of what might be considered a 'developmentally appropriate material' is difficult to judge from the outside, as learners we all have unique ways of seeing and understanding the world that may or may not be unlocked by given representations.

ACTIVITY

Consider when you have tried to learn something new (perhaps something that is obviously 'mathematical' or perhaps something where the maths is less overt, such as cooking or driving, or building flat pack furniture...). What do you consider your depth of understanding of this to be? Do you understand why or how it 'works'? Which representations were most or least helpful? Why?

The ideas that each child ought to progress through the use of these representations seems to be one of the most visible demonstrations of the idea that maths is a 'building block' subject, as discussed in the introduction to chapters 1–3. There is a danger that the use of manipulatives and pictures can, within the hierarchical learning culture that results from this view, become associated with not being able to do maths 'properly' or not being as good at it as others who are able to work more abstractly before us. It could encourage unhelpful comparisons, particularly if there is a distorted sense of a standardised timescale within with children 'ought' to be moving on, or up, through this hierarchy. Should children be working abstractly by the end of their Reception year, or the end of Key Stage 1, or the end of Key Stage 2, or 3... or do elements of non-abstract representations retain their relevance into mathematical learning beyond even these stages? Indeed, principles from cognitive science acknowledge that 'Progress in using more efficient (arithmetic) strategies is likely to be non-linear and gradual' (Deans for Impact, 2019, p. 14).

We suggest that it is more helpful for children to see all representations as of equal value when exploring ideas and that it could be better to develop conversations about what best serves the mathematics in hand, and the communication of those ideas depending on the context. This is undoubtedly more complex; it requires a commitment to accept and work with that complexity not least through a continued willingness to develop our own mathematical thinking. Ultimately though, a layered, interconnected approach to each child's interaction with mathematical representations has the potential to unlock the subject in more satisfying ways for everyone.

POSITIVE RELATIONSHIPS

The relationship between 'feeling' and 'seeing' mathematics in the context of positive relationships is so closely interwoven with ideas connected to the unique child and enabling environments that teasing out specific elements is difficult. However, one of the topics that is most pertinent to this is the use (or not) of fingers...

While the debate around children's use of fingers in mathematics can fall into a false dichotomy, either fingers = good or fingers = bad, there is an increasing awareness of *how* and *when* they might be effectively utilised to support mathematical learning, with national programmes such as the NCETM's 'Mastering Number' overtly incorporating them into daily Reception maths learning (e.g. see their 'grow, show, throw' activity in the 'Cardinality and Number Sense' resource below). Again, there is support from cognitive science research for the benefits of using fingers (Deans for Impact, 2019) not least as it helps to reduce cognitive load through the incorporation of gesture alongside speech (Goldin-Meadow et al., 2001). Sarama and Clements (2009) draw on a range of research to argue that using fingers in arithmetic results in an acceleration of competence with single digit addition and subtraction. They also warn against attempts to stop children using their fingers too soon.

Positive relationships and the use of representations in maths can therefore largely be understood through the need to ensure that no harm is done to children's perception of themselves as mathematical learners through overtly negative judgements of the ways in which they 'feel' and 'see' the subject, or any of its component parts. Our responses to their chosen or preferred representations need to be framed as cooperative explorations about what is most useful or helpful and ensure that enjoyment and success is a top priority.

ACTIVITY

Make a list of all the action songs and rhymes that you can think of (or find!) that incorporate number and gesture, including finger use. Can you remember any from your own childhood?

ENABLING ENVIRONMENTS

There are a plethora of texts and websites that offer ideas of specific resources that need to be included in learning environments to offer access to a range of mathematical representations of number, both as part of continuous and enhanced provision, and for guided learning opportunities – some of our favourites are listed at the end of this chapter.

The importance of 'feeling' and 'seeing' mathematics does not only apply to developing understanding of an abstract number system but also to statistics, measures and geometry. We might support the development of statistical thinking by enhancing provision through sorting provocations; these could be applied to any group of objects and is especially useful at 'tidy up time'! We might encourage the comparison of sets to begin ideas of representing and interpreting data, or of using such data to answer questions and solve problems. Measurement apparatus for length, weight (mass), capacity and time can offer meaningful contexts for core conceptual understanding about scale, number order, part-whole relationships and comparison. Many concrete and pictorial resources will support geometrical learning as they encourage the combining and separating of 3D and 2D shapes (although please remember, if you can pick it up, it's 3D – even if it is thin! 2D shapes are visible purely as pictures, or on the faces of 3D shapes). Again, some of our favourites for this such as pattern blocks and tangrams are in the 'Further Reading/Resources' section below. Other resources such as building blocks and empty packaging including *big* blocks and cardboard boxes are also crucial for 'feeling' and 'seeing' shape and space. However, when exploring effective provision for learning about shape, some key knowledge about the variety of examples we provide is crucial.

VARIETY OF EXAMPLES

We must remember that children are interacting with shapes from birth, and we need to build on this knowledge with explorations about properties that deepen geometrical understanding, rather than offering '...relatively low-quality name learning activities' (Tucker, 2014, p. 77). We also need to consider how we draw on the reality of how shapes are presented in the world, often irregular, in different orientations, or as 'almost' shapes, e.g. triangles visible in playground equipment that have rounded edges, or 'bumpy' sides during maths trails or shape hunts. When considering what constitutes an enabling environment for learning about shape, we need to consider variety in order that children do not form narrow and limiting views that could ultimately lead to confusion, frustration and boredom as they progress in their mathematical learning. We have lost count of the number of tricky situations we have had to navigate with student teachers when they meet the idea that a square is also a rectangle for the first time...

ACTIVITY

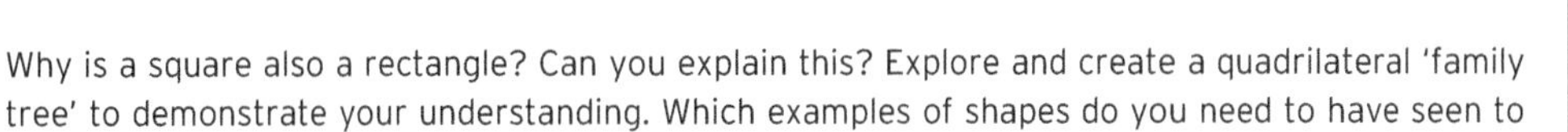

Why is a square also a rectangle? Can you explain this? Explore and create a quadrilateral 'family tree' to demonstrate your understanding. Which examples of shapes do you need to have seen to develop your thinking around this geometrical knowledge?

When providing resources and activities that support children to 'feel' and 'see' shapes, we need to offer those which draw attention to their critical attributes, '... a critical attribute is a characteristic shared by all examples of a shape' (Clements,

2020). So, for example, we might want to offer examples of different sizes, colours, number of sides, length of sides and orientation, as demonstrated in the image of 2D shapes below (Figure 5.2).

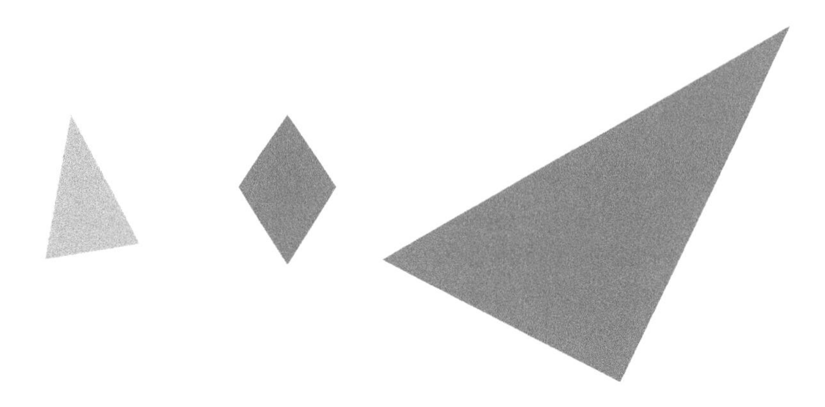

Figure 5.2

Features such as colour and size are transient properties of shape, so as educators, we need to consider how we get children to focus on the mathematical properties. Showing a collection of shapes such as these and asking them to consider which is the odd one out will enable us to explore these transient and critical attributes. Such 'odd one out' activities can be used as part of guided learning or enhanced provision, with shapes available for children to continue this into their free play. This is equally applicable to learning about 3D shapes.

Often the examples of 2D shapes that are deliberately displayed in an Early Years environment, on posters or display boards, include a single prototypical representation of common shapes: a square, a rectangle, a circle, an equilateral triangle and perhaps regular pentagons and hexagons, all of which are presented (where applicable) on a horizontal base. There is no expectation set for which specific shapes children might explore in the Early Years although there seems to be a sense that some shapes are 'easier' or 'simpler' than others. We suggest that this viewpoint may be limiting the opportunities for children to develop creative and critical thinking that a deep exploration of shape can offer.

ACTIVITY

Consider the image below (Figure 5.3).

How long does it take you to find the pentagons? How do you know which ones the pentagons are? Which attributes are you drawn to considering? How deep is your understanding of what the critical attributes of a pentagon are?

(Continued)

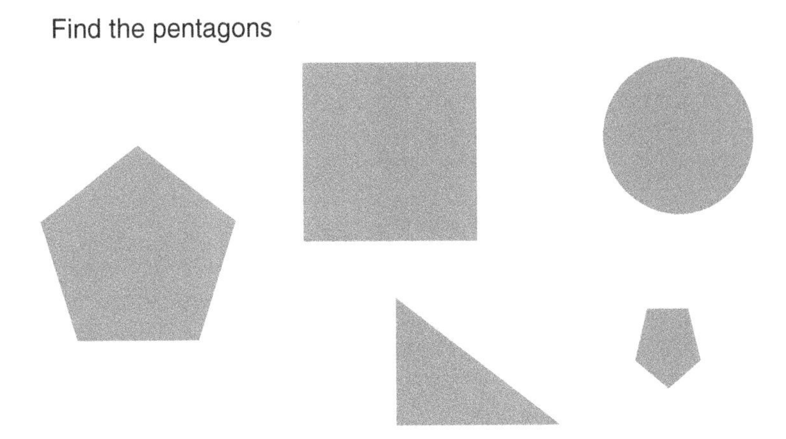

Figure 5.3

Now, study the image below and consider the same questions (Figure 5.4).

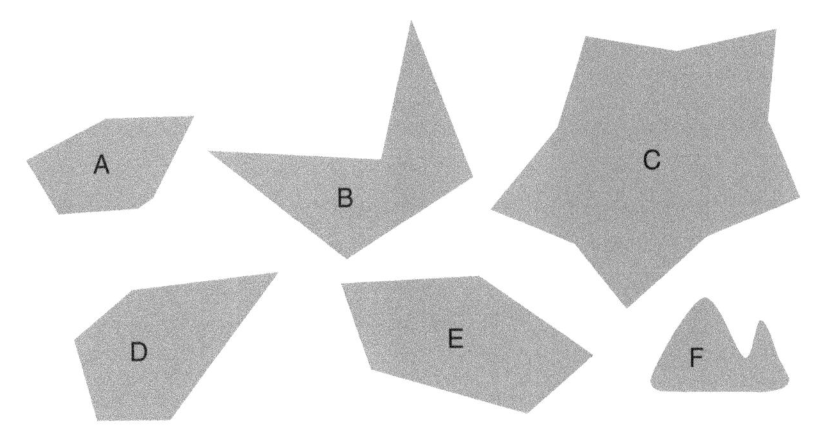

Figure 5.4

How long does it take you to find the pentagons this time? How do you know which ones the pentagons are? Which attributes are you drawn to considering? How deep is your understanding of what the critical attributes of a pentagon are? Do you have any further questions...?

The carefully considered examples in Figure 5.4 enable learners to distinguish the features of what it means to be a pentagon. You will have noticed the carefully chosen 'almost' or 'non-examples'; let's explore each example and why they have been included:

- Shape A is actually a hexagon, but the really short side may be overlooked or discounted by the children as if it is not relevant. If children are only used to seeing shapes with the same length sides, presenting shapes with a significant difference in the length of the sides will be beneficial.

(Continued)

(Continued)

- Shape B has an 'inverted corner' which is great to spark discussion. Do the children consider it to be a corner? What is it that makes a corner a corner? What we see is in fact two straight sides meeting at a point, so yes, this is a corner. If we use a definition of a pentagon to be '5 sides and 5 corners' then this meets the criteria. However, we can discuss the differences between the interior angles of this *concave* pentagon (one of which is greater than 180°) versus those of a *convex* pentagon (all of the interior angles are less than 180°). While we might not expect our Early Years learners to use this language, they might notice the difference and be supported to articulate what they see.
- Shape C, the star, has a five-ness about it, it has five 'points' which children may consider to be five corners (especially if they discount the 'inverted corners' discussed in relation to shape B).
- Shape D is quite close to a prototypical image of a pentagon and is presented on a horizontal base, but it is altered enough to make you double check!
- Shape E is the closest to a prototypical pentagon, but even then, it is not a regular pentagon, and is not presented on a horizontal base. Children may instantly recognise it as a pentagon, but through this we still extend the range of images and examples that form their concept of what a pentagon looks like.
- Shape F is an interesting one! Here we are looking to see if the children have understood the fundamental idea that for a shape to belong in the pentagon family it must be a polygon, i.e. have straight sides.

What we see in the examples in this last image is not just variety, but what is known as *variation* which is a core element of mathematical learning connected to the examples we are given to think about. According to the NCETM (2020), 'the central idea of teaching with variation is to highlight the essential features of a concept or idea through varying the non-essential features (and) Variation is not the same as variety – careful attention needs to be paid to what aspects are being varied (and what is not being varied) and for what purpose'. The examples of shapes in the environment, and arguably of all mathematical concepts, should therefore support children to learn 'what it is' by simultaneously building a deeper understanding of 'what it is not' in detailed and nuanced ways (Lo, 2013).

The role of the adult in supporting children to 'feel' and 'see' the mathematics is key in both the knowledgeable provision of mathematically interesting and appropriate resources, and in the provocations and skilful interactions that develop sustained shared thinking (Purdon, 2016). It is the role that resources have in developing play and exploration, active learning, and critical and creative thinking that matters most as '...understanding does not travel through the fingertips and up the arm...' (Ball, 1992 in Clements and Sarama, 2018, p. 73). The ways in which this might be developed further are explored in more detail in Chapter 6: 'How are we talking?'.

SUMMARY

If we return to the Early Years Foundation Stage (EYFS) specific areas for learning and development, we can see how much is, both explicitly and implicitly, related to the ability to 'feel' and 'see' mathematics.

> *Developing a strong grounding in number is essential so that all children develop the necessary building blocks to excel mathematically. Children should be able to count confidently,* ***develop a deep understanding of the numbers to 10, the relationships between them and the patterns within those numbers. By providing frequent and varied opportunities to build and apply this understanding – such as using manipulatives, including small pebbles and tens frames for organising counting – children will develop a secure base of knowledge*** *and vocabulary from which mastery of mathematics is built. In addition,* ***it is important that the curriculum includes rich opportunities for children to develop their spatial reasoning skills across all areas of mathematics including shape, space and measures.*** *It is important that children develop positive attitudes and interests in mathematics,* ***look for patterns and relationships, spot connections, 'have a go', talk to adults and peers about what they notice and not be afraid to make mistakes.***
>
> (DfE, 2021)

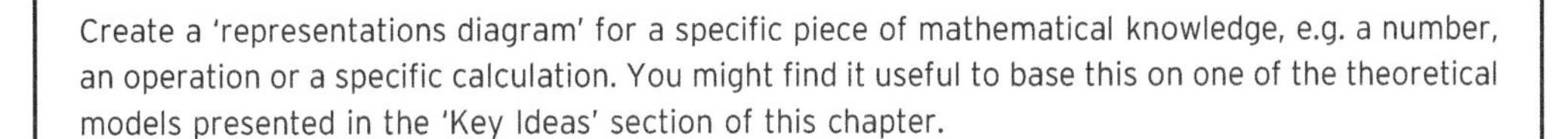

Create a 'representations diagram' for a specific piece of mathematical knowledge, e.g. a number, an operation or a specific calculation. You might find it useful to base this on one of the theoretical models presented in the 'Key Ideas' section of this chapter.

This chapter has discussed key theories and practices around this core element of effective mathematics provision, the opportunity to 'feel' and 'see' mathematics. The connections that can be made between the varying ways in which mathematics is represented have been explored, as well as the ways in which information might be broken down and built up into interconnected and layered webs of meaning about fundamental mathematical concepts (Russell, 2000). Haylock and Cockburn (2017) provide a useful example of what this might look like in summary:

> *They make connections between concrete experience and language when they relate their manipulation of the toy cars to the language patterns of '...shared between ... is*

> *... each', and 'sets of ... make ... altogether'. They connect their concrete experience with a picture of three sets of two things. The language of their sentences is connected with the symbols on the keys and display of the calculator. And then, later, they will be learning to connect these opportunities to make so many connections between language, concrete experience, pictures and symbols that we would recognise this as an activity promoting mathematical understanding.*
>
> (p. 13)

FURTHER READING/RESOURCES

Back, J. (2018a). *Early number sense.* https://nrich.maths.org/10737

Back, J. (2018b). *Place value: The ten-ness of ten.*

BBC. (2022). *Numberblocks.*

Bird, R. (2013a). *Exploring numbers through dot patterns.* Ronit Bird.

Bird, R. (2013b). *Exploring numbers through cuisenaire rods.* Ronit Bird.

Bird, R. (2022). Games and resources, including dice, domino and card games. http://www.ronitbird.com/games/

Frykholm, J. (2008). *Learning to think mathematically with the Rekenrek: A resource for teachers, a tool for young children.* The Math Learning Center. https://www.mathlearningcenter.org/sites/default/files/pdfs/LTM_Rekenrek.pdf

Gregg, S. (2020). *Pattern blocks book and templates.* ATM. https://www.atm.org.uk/Shop/Pattern-Blocks-book-and-slides/ACT123pk

NCETM. (2020). *Cardinality and number sense.* https://www.ncetm.org.uk/features/cardinality-and-number-sense

Nrich. (2022). *Tangram pictures.* https://nrich.maths.org/715

Ollerton, M., Williams, H., & Gregg, S. (2017). *Cuisenaire – From early years to adult.* ATM.

Swan, P. (2022). *Pattern blocks.* http://mathsmaterials.com/pattern-blocks/

Woodham, L., & Pennant, J. (2018). *How can I support the development of early number sense and place value? Age 3 to 11.* https://nrich.maths.org/10739

REFERENCES

Askew, M. (2018). *Models in mind.* NRICH. https://nrich.maths.org/8348

Aubrey, C. (1997). *Mathematics teaching in the early years: An investigation of teachers' subject knowledge.* Falmer Press.

Bruner, J. (1966). *Toward a theory of instruction.* Belknapp Press.

Clements, D. (2020). *Early childhood math: Geometry, patterns, measurements, and data analysis.* https://www.youtube.com/watch?v=YEPdXRbI5Xc

ClementsD., & SaramaJ. (2018). Myths of early math. *Education Sciences, 8*(2), 71–78.

Deans for Impact. (2019). *The science of early learning.* Austin, TX: Deans for Impact.

DfE. (2021). *EYFS framework.* https://assets.publishing.service.gov.uk/government/uploads/system/uploads/attachment_data/file/974907/EYFS_framework_-_March_2021.pdf

Gardner, A. F., & Jones, B. D. (2016). Examining the Reggio Emilia approach: Keys to understanding why it motivates students, *Electronic Journal of Research in Educational Psychology, 14*(3), 602–625.

Goldin-Meadow, S., Kelly, S., Nusbaum, H., & Wagner Cook, S. (2001). Explaining math: Gesturing lightens the load. *Psychological Science, 12*(6), 516–522.

Haylock, D., & Cockburn, A. (2017). *Understanding mathematics for young children: A guide for teachers of children (Vols. 3–7).* Los Angeles: SAGE.

Lakoff, G., & Nunez, R. E. (2000). *Where mathematics comes from: How the embodied mind brings mathematics into being.* Basic Books.

Liebeck, P. (1990). *How children learn mathematics: A guide for parents and teachers.* London: Penguin.

Lo, M. L. (2013). Variation theory and the improvement of teaching and learning. *International Journal for Lesson and Learning Studies, 2*(2), 188–195.

NCETM. (2020). *Variation.* https://www.ncetm.org.uk/media/8d85bba06845025/variation_handout_september_2020.pdf

Purdon, A. (2016). Sustained shared thinking in an early childhood setting: An exploration of practitioners' perspectives. *International Journal of Primary, Elementary and Early Years Education, 44*(3), 269–282.

Russell, S. J. (2000). Developing computational fluency with whole numbers. *Teaching Children Mathematics, 7*(3), 154–158.

Sarama, J., & Clements, D. (2009). *Early childhood mathematics education research: Learning trajectories for young children*. Routledge.

Skemp, R. (2006). Relational understanding and instrumental understanding. *Mathematics Teaching in the Middle School, 12*(2), 88–95.

Tucker, K. (2014). *Mathematics through play in the early years*. SAGE.

Woodham, L., & Pennant, J. (2018). *How can I support the development of early number sense and Place value? Age 3 to 11*. https://nrich.maths.org/10739

6

HOW ARE WE TALKING?

CHAPTER OBJECTIVES

- Consider the importance of developing mathematical vocabulary
- Develop knowledge of strategies for developing mathematical vocabulary
- Explore strategies for developing high-quality dialogue
- Develop knowledge and understanding of effective questioning strategies for mathematical thinking

INTRODUCTION

The central role of 'maths talk' to effective mathematical learning is undeniable and well-documented in the field of early education; it is fundamental to the prime area of the Early Years Foundation Stage (EYFS) 'language and communication' and undoubtedly has a key part to play in 'personal, social and emotional development'. It can be defined as the use of spoken language to discuss and participate in dialogue that goes beyond an exchange of words to the development of meaning (Harrison, 2007). It is one of the primary ways in which thoughts and ideas, knowledge and skills are shared, and a cornerstone upon which relationships are built and learning cultures are created. This chapter will provide you with strategies for how these prime areas can be strengthened and applied in the specific area of mathematics. It is deliberately titled 'How are *we* talking?' in order to highlight a planning focus on the ways in which talk is accessed and used by all participants in the learning process, both children and adults, and how the quality of each interaction can be enhanced.

Again, your approach to 'maths talk' in your setting will be influenced by your beliefs about how children learn, how children learn *maths* and what maths is. It is therefore useful to spend some time reflecting on your own experiences of talk in your own mathematical learning, and in your experiences with children.

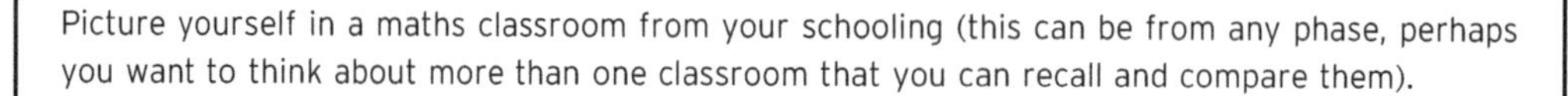

ACTIVITY

Picture yourself in a maths classroom from your schooling (this can be from any phase, perhaps you want to think about more than one classroom that you can recall and compare them).

- Are you talking? Who is talking?
- When do you talk?
- What do you talk about?
- Can you understand what is said to you?
- Can you make yourself and your thinking understood?
- How do you feel about the subject as a result of the type of talk that is going on?

Now reflect on your experience(s) through the lens of the principles for Early Years practice:

- To what extent were your communication needs as a 'unique child' met?
- Did you have any positive relationships as a result of talking? With whom? What made them positive?
- In what ways did your environment support your/others 'maths talk'?

How might these experiences have influenced your own use of maths talk as an adult/Early Years educator?

KEY IDEAS

Inevitably, 'talk' overlaps with each of the other four elements for maths planning. Playful and purposeful mathematical experiences will give rise to opportunities for talk, talk is integral to creating meaning and therefore developing purposeful mathematical learning. Showing the maths through a range of representations both provokes talk and clarifies meaning, and maths talk provides an opportunity for connection to and application of the prime areas of communication and language and personal, social and emotional development.

The EYFS (DfE, 2021) for mathematics states that children should 'talk to adults and peers about what they notice' but this simplistic statement does not do justice to the complexities and necessity of talk to mathematical learning. Subject-specific vocabulary, dialogue and questioning are three core aspects for consideration when planning for how talk will be incorporated into early maths provision.

SUBJECT-SPECIFIC VOCABULARY

> *There is an increasing number of teachers of mathematics who know not only that the language in the classroom matters in general, but that there are peculiarly mathematical language problems.*
>
> (Brookes et al., 1991, preface)

ACTIVITY

What is the first thing that comes to mind when you see each of the following words?

1. Face
2. Volume
3. Side
4. Depth
5. Take away

These are just some examples of when maths vocabulary has a different meaning to its everyday use in English. Talking about the face of a clock or the face of a 3D shape may confuse the learner who is connecting the word face with what looks back at them in the mirror! Similarly, children who are used to connecting volume with sound will need to understand its mathematical role defining how much space something takes up. Depth might be related to swimming pools while the many different connotations of 'sides' (inside, outside, teams playing against each other, a side of a coin, etc.) can all distract from its mathematical definition as the straight edge of a 2D shape. These are just some examples of language that are subject-specific and part of a learner's disciplinary/content literacy, classified as 'Tier 3' words by Beck et al. (2013).

The EYFS (DfE, 2021) states that 'children will develop a secure base of knowledge and vocabulary from which mastery of mathematics is built'. This 'secure base of vocabulary' relies on the timely introduction of unfamiliar words to allow for exploration and clarification. These are key, as adult insistence that the 'right' word is used without links to actions, processes, objects and/or symbols is likely to lead to superficial or confused learning (Bird, 1991; Haylock & Cockburn, 2013). In order to support this learning of vocabulary with meaning, a mastery approach (as summarised in Chapter 1) advocates the habitualisation of speaking in full sentences in response to specific, vocabulary-reliant questions to develop useful language patterns (Drury, 2014; Haylock & Cockburn, 2013).

DIALOGIC TALK

Dialogue is one example of talk which has the specific purpose to 'build up shared understanding through structured, challenging yet reciprocated talk' (Alexander, 2001, pp. 1–2). In practice, the term 'discussion' might be used synonymously with dialogue, but in terms of formal definition, the combination of conversation with the advancement of an inquiry through the skilful framing of questions and constructing of answers which 'dialogue' offers is considered more relevant in mathematical learning.

This form of dialogic talk has its roots in Vygotsky's socio-cultural model of education, whereby

> *students develop higher mental functions through mediated, social and collaborative activity...(and) move their dependency on explicit forms of mediation to more implicit forms such as inner speech, shifting their dependency on others towards an independence associated with remembering, internalising and using cultural tools.*
>
> (Walshaw, 2017, p. 294)

According to Alexander (2008), the main elements required to facilitate high-quality dialogue are:

- interactions which encourage students to think and to think in different ways;
- questions which invite much more than simple recall;
- answers which are justified, followed up and built upon rather than merely received;
- feedback which informs and leads thinking forward as well as encourages;
- contributions which are extended rather than fragmented;
- exchanges which chain together into coherent and deepening lines of enquiry;

- discussion and argumentation which probe and challenge rather than unquestioningly accept;
- professional engagement with subject matter which liberates classroom discourse from the safe and conventional;
- classroom organisation, climate and relationships which make all this possible.

The application of this model for talk into early education takes the form of 'sustained shared thinking' (Gifford, 2008; Purdon, 2016) which focuses on discussion that seeks to establish understanding through the solving of a problem, clarification of a concept, evaluation of an activity or the extension of a narrative (Siraj-Blatchford, 2009).

QUESTIONING

Questions are an integral part of 'maths talk' for learning not only in terms of those posed by adults to support thinking and evaluate learning but also in terms of those generated by the children themselves which provide clues about their current interests, knowledge and understanding (Bird, 1991). Those asked by adults will include closed, open and indirect questions, and are likely to develop higher-order thinking skills if they encourage focus, explanation, prediction and speculation (Gifford, 2008). However, we must be aware that questions can inadvertently shut down children's contributions to dialogue as they can be perceived as a test of what is known, rather than an invitation to participate and so 'always/sometimes/never true' statements also have value (Askew, 2012; Gifford, 2008).

UNIQUE CHILD

When considering the unique child in the context of maths talk, one key tension to be negotiated is related to subject-specific vocabulary around a potential 'language gap' between each child's informal language and the formalised mathematical terms. Children will use their prior experiences and informal language to make sense of ideas and communicate their thinking, but this might not always draw on mathematical words or phrases. As adults, our response needs to balance an honouring of the child's word-choice with refining their knowledge and use of technical vocabulary in order that they can better access the mathematics 'register' and perceive themselves as a mathematician (Drury, 2014). The EYFS (DfE, 2021) states, 'by...echoing back what they say with new vocabulary added practitioners will build children's language effectively', or as one Infant School headteacher put it, 'You take this precious thing (word) they give you, look at it, polish it up and hand it back to them'.

CASE STUDY

Charlotte is using thin 3D shapes to create a picture of towers 'for spiderman to swing between'. She starts to name the 2D shapes she can see on the faces as she is looking for them in the central pile, 'I need another square, where is a square, that one is too small...'. She then selects a shape with hexagonal faces and says to the adult nearby, 'This one is like a circle...' and the adult responds by saying, 'Yes, it is like a circle, but it's got straight sides... How many sides has it got (counts, Charlotte joins in) . . . six, that means it's a hexagon. Can you find any more hexagons?'. Charlotte searches for similar shapes saying 'hexagon...hexagon...there's one, and another one, I've got three hexagons now!'.

ACTIVITY

Jot down all the vocabulary that could be associated with teaching the four operations (addition, subtraction, multiplication and division).*

Now consider the pros and cons of introducing children to the range of vocabulary you have noted.

Can you draw on your experience of children in the Early Years to identify some examples of informal language and suggest how these could be understood and then 'polished' to develop more formal vocabulary?

*NB. Although calculating with the four operations does not officially appear until Key Stage 1, children in the Early Years will naturally be engaged with some maths relating to these in their play and daily activities.

Another consideration regarding 'talk' and the unique child is related to questioning. Firstly, we need to consider how much scope we give for children's own questions to arise and be considered. Haylock and Cockburn (2013) suggest providing opportunities for children to make up as many different questions as they can about a particular situation (snack time, playing in the park, travelling to school).

Secondly, our adult responses to children's questions need to take into account the uniqueness of each child in the avoidance of assumptions when ascribing intention or meaning (Bird, 1991), to what extent do we respond to what we *think* we have heard or to what we *want* to have heard and bend children's questions towards our adult-led agenda? 'Tuning-in' to what each child is really asking us is challenging in the busy, demanding context of Early Years education, but an effort to actively listen, to see things as they are seeing them, is essential if we are to interact effectively and ensure high-quality mathematical learning experiences for each unique child (Coleyshaw et al., 2010; Webb, 2018).

POSITIVE RELATIONSHIPS

An appreciation for the unique child's perspective is also integral to the development of positive relationships, and how adults and children talk with each other in mathematical learning can have a significant influence on such relationships.

Adults can demonstrate 'care' for learners *and* for maths itself by ensuring that dialogue demonstrates mutual respect through an emphasis on listening, a willingness to follow a developmentally appropriate pace and pitch of learning and coming alongside children to share the storytelling of their learning (Watson, 2021). Conversation is participated in with a full awareness of the power dynamic that exists between adults and children and a conscious effort to have authentic conversations that value all contributions equally, avoiding the 'guess what's in my head' game that tacitly limits and controls learners' thinking (Bagnall, 2013). This is not to reduce an adult's authority in terms of expertise, we will guide mathematical conversations, offer new vocabulary, and identify and correct errors and misconceptions of course, but more to remind us that in terms of being 'the person in charge' we need to underplay our role when talking with children (Bird, 1991).

Some suggestions for how we might achieve this are listed below:

- **Give yourself time** to authentically listen to learners' talk, and avoid making assumptions about what is being said
- **Give the child time** to formulate their thoughts and words and respond at their own speed
- **Share the power** by monitoring your intonation and body language and relinquishing your control of the talk, avoid responses that prioritise your own agenda
- **Don't rush to 'rescue'** when something is wrong, prioritise remaining curious about what *they* are thinking through speculative comments e.g. 'I wonder why...?', 'What could you try instead?', 'What do you think?'
- **Support community talk** through modelling and guiding child–child conversation, or providing a toy or puppet to talk through/to

(Adapted from the work of Bagnall, 2013; Bird, 1991¿Gifford, 2008)

In order to encourage positive relationships between learners, it can also be useful to have some guidelines for mathematical exploratory talk (Mercer, 2008) that could include:

- ask questions
- respect everyone's ideas and opinions
- challenge the idea, not the person
- give reasons for your answers
- work out how you can agree if a decision needs to be made.

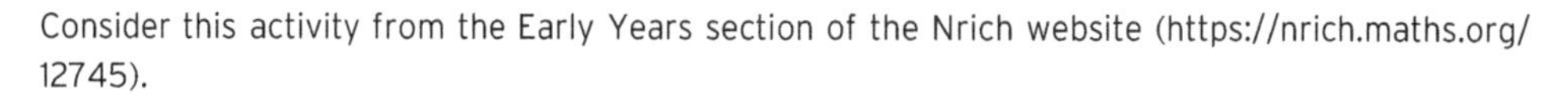

ACTIVITY

Consider this activity from the Early Years section of the Nrich website (https://nrich.maths.org/12745).

The Box Game:

Put toys one at a time into the box, so children cannot see them inside, counting all together. Ask: 'Can you show on your fingers how many are hidden?' Display a large numeral.

Add one to the box, without showing the objects inside, and ask children to show on their fingers, 'How many are there now?'. Then show how many are inside the box and count to check.

How could this activity be adapted to develop the mathematical talk and ensure positive relationships are encouraged (child-adult, child-child, child-mathematics...)?

ENABLING ENVIRONMENTS

The role of the adult is key in enabling mathematical talk with the aim of supporting mathematical thinking and understanding, what later in the primary curriculum becomes classified as 'reasoning'. The following examples of the ways in which adults might interact with children to develop 'shared sustained thinking' are appropriate and applicable to both guided teaching/learning opportunities and 'teachable moments' as part of enhanced and continuous provision.

Within a culture of positive relationships, it can be helpful for adults to consider a range of questions and prompts that promote and provoke specifically mathematical thinking. Watson and Mason (1998) list a range of mental activity and collated them into six categories which can be simplified as exemplifying, correcting, comparing, changing, generalising and explaining. Below is a list of questions and prompts, based on their work, which could be useful in early mathematics learning.

Exemplifying	Describe, Demonstrate, Tell, Show, Choose, Draw, Can you find an(other) example of...? Is...an example of...? What makes...an example of...? Can you find something that *isn't* an example of...?
Correcting	Tell me what is wrong with... What needs to be changed so that...?
Comparing	What is the same and different about...? Can you sort...according to...? Is it or is it not...? Can you prove yourself wrong? What matters most/least?
Changing	What do you get if you change...? What if...? What other questions would have the same answer? Can you do this in more than one way? What is the quickest, easiest...?
Generalising	Is it always, sometimes, never...? What are all the possible ways to...? What can change and what has to stay the same so that... is still true? Is there a pattern? Is there a rule?
Explaining	Why is that right/wrong? Can you convince me that you're right? How can we be sure that...? Tell me what is wrong with... Is it always true that...?

We might also support the early verbalisation of mathematical reasoning through the modelling and provision of sentence starters such as,

- 'It can't be because...'
- 'It must be because...'
- 'This is always true because...'
- 'This is true here because...'

- 'I already know that... so...'
- 'If... then...'
- 'This is the same because...'
- 'This is different because...'

Questions for assessing and reflecting on the mathematical learning are also a key part of an effective learning environment, examples of which might be:

Assessment	What have you discovered? How did you find that out? Why do you think that? What made you decide to do it that way?
Reflection	Who has the same answer/pattern/grouping as this? Who has a different solution? Are everybody's results the same? Why/why not? Have we found all the possibilities? How do we know? Have you thought of another way this could be done? Do you think we have found the best solution?

(Way, 2014)

The mathematical tasks and activities provided in the learning environment form another crucial strand in the development of high-quality talk, and there are many and varied resources and texts available that are entirely devoted to collections of these, many of which are explored in Chapter 4: 'Is it playful?'. However, when planning for playful practice to encourage talk, it is worth considering the use of storybooks and role-play as rich inspirations and contexts for the development of mathematical talk. This is also explored in more detail in Chapter 7: 'What is it connected to?'.

Finally, 'Number Talks' are 'classroom conversations focused on making sense of mathematics' (Parrish, 2014, p. 203) that are underpinned by the core principles of developing a culture of community learning, facilitating the learner's construction of meaning and honouring current understanding while encouraging refinement of mathematical knowledge, understanding and skills. In early maths, they are often based on discussions about dot patterns or rekenrek images that are explored further in Chapter 5: 'Can we feel it and see it?'. The inclusion of number talks in children's early experiences of maths supports the development of fluency and reasoning as they encourage flexible and efficient ways of 'seeing' and articulating thinking about number.

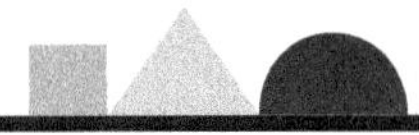

ACTIVITY

Explore the 'Number Talks' activity for Early Years found on the NRICH website https://nrich.maths.org/14005

Try it out, either with a child/group of children, or with friends/family! How does the structure of the activity encourage high-quality mathematical talk? How could these principles be applied to other such activities?

SUMMARY

These benefits of effective talk are summed up concisely by Askew (2012), who explains:

> *Much talk in mathematics lessons stops short at children sharing their finished methods. The emphasis is on children reporting already complete mathematics and the talk resembles a series of monologues, with one child offering their solution followed by another. The other class members are cast as passive listeners, or, at best, good listeners, which usually means looking attentive and not interrupting. Children need to be active listeners, attending to and then attuning to the messages from their peers and becoming mindful of connections with their own emergent understandings and mathematical voice. Where speaking and listening are both well established in classroom activity, dialogue can occur in which mathematical ideas are invoked, arranged, expressed, and played with until the collective understanding is well pitched. When pupils are attuned to and thinking about each other's methods then it is possible that a dialogue unfolds about the relative benefits of different methods and, say, which are more effective, rather than simply whether or not they are correct. Mathematical meaning emerges through giving voice to tasks and tools: without talk mathematical images are silent, like notes on a sheet of music. Musicians know the difference between printed notes and live music. Mathematicians know the difference between written symbols and doing maths. Learning mathematics is coming to know this difference. Talk is how we come to that knowing.*
>
> (p. 128)

ACTIVITY

Choose one aspect of the EYFS framework for mathematics and write down how you would plan for the mathematical talk it entails.

Consider:

- What might the children need to see or hear to aid the vocabulary development?
- How might you ensure the dialogue allows for the child(ren) to lead the conversation?
- What questions or prompts might you plan to use that are relevant to the focus of the learning?
- Does your thinking change in the context of continuous/enhanced/guided provision?

FURTHER READING/RESOURCES

Chapter 11, 'Talk', in Transforming Primary Mathematics by Mike Askew (2012)

Sustained shared thinking and communication pedagogies

- https://earlymaths.org/early-years-mathematics-pedagogy-exploration-apprenticeship-making-sense/
- https://early-education.org.uk/sustained-shared-thinking-sst/

Ideas for effective interaction in mathematics learning. https://nzmaths.co.nz/supporting-rich-mathematical-interactions-ece

Key stage one research project into the application of dialogic teaching in mathematics. http://www.talkmathstalk.co.uk/

Maths through stories. https://www.mathsthroughstories.org/

REFERENCES

Alexander, R. J. (2001). *Culture and pedagogy: International comparisons in primary education*. Blackwell.

Alexander, R. J. (2008). *Towards dialogic teaching: Rethinking classroom talk* (4th ed.). Dialogos.

Askew, M. (2012). *Transforming primary mathematics*. Routledge.

Bagnall, B. (2013). *What's all the talking about?* NRICH. https://nrich.maths.org/6662

Beck, I., McKeown, M. G., & Kucan, L. (2013). *Bringing words to life* (2nd ed.). New York, NY: Guilford Press.

Bird, M. H. (1991). *Mathematics for young children*. Routledge.

Brookes, B., Dichmont, J., Love, E., Morgan, J., Tahta, D., & Thorpe, J. (1991). *Towards a language of struggle*. ATM. https://www.atm.org.uk/write/MediaUploads/Shop%20Images/Look%20Inside/DNL040.pdf

Coleyshaw, L., Whitmarsh, J., Jopling, M., & Hadfield, M. (2010). *Listening to children's perspectives: Improving the quality of provision in early years settings*. DfE. https://assets.publishing.service.gov.uk/government/uploads/system/uploads/attachment_data/file/183412/DfE-RR239b_report.pdf

DfE. (2021). *Statutory framework for the early years foundation stage*. https://assets.publishing.service.gov.uk/government/uploads/system/uploads/attachment_data/file/974907/EYFS_framework_-_March_2021.pdf

Drury, H. (2014). *Mastering mathematics: Teaching to transform achievement*. Oxford University Press.

Gifford, S. (2008). *Teaching mathematics 3-5*. Open University Press.

Harrison, C. (2007). Banishing the quiet classroom. *Education Review, 19*(2), 67–77.

Haylock, D., & Cockburn, A. (2013). *Understanding mathematics for young children*. SAGE.

Mercer, N. (2008). *Exploring talk in school*. SAGE.

Parrish, S. (2014). *Number talks: Whole number computation: Grades K-5*. Math Solutions.

Purdon, A. (2016). Sustained shared thinking in an early childhood setting: An exploration of practitioners' perspectives. *International Journal of Primary, Elementary and Early Years Education, 44*(3), 269–282.

Siraj-BlatchfordI. (2009). Conceptualising progression in the pedagogy of play and sustained shared thinking in early childhood education: A Vygotskian perspective. *Education and Child Psychology, 26*(2), 77–89.

Walshaw, M. (2017). Understanding mathematical development through Vygotsky. *Research in Mathematics Education, 19*(3), 293–309. https://doi.org/10.1080/14794802.2017.1379728

Watson, A. (2021). *Care, MT* (Vol. *279*, pp. 11–15). ATM.

Watson, A., & Mason, J. (1998). *Questions and prompts for mathematical thinking*. ATM.

Way, J. (2014). *Using questioning to stimulate mathematical thinking*. NRICH. https://nrich.maths.org/2473

Webb, P. (2018). *Listening to the children, early years educator*. https://www.earlyyearseducator.co.uk/features/article/listening-to-the-children

7

WHAT IS IT CONNECTED TO?

CHAPTER OBJECTIVES

- Consider the relevance of mathematics across other areas of the Early Years Foundation Stage (EYFS).
- Explore how a range of opportunities can be used to develop mathematical learning, thinking and understanding.

INTRODUCTION

There are two main perspectives to consider as we think about 'connections' when we talk about mathematics: connections within mathematics as a subject and connections beyond the subject of mathematics.

When considering connections within mathematics, two main ideas are prevalent: connections to prior learning and connections across areas of mathematics. Making connections to prior learning ties in with a mastery approach, knowing what the building blocks for a concept are and ensuring firm foundations in children's learning. Identifying connections across mathematics enables learners to see that we can apply our understanding of one aspect of mathematics (i.e. place value) to help us understand other areas (such as reading scales on graphs or measuring equipment). We sometimes like to use a jigsaw analogy for this; we encourage learners to see how different areas of mathematics connect to complete a 'bigger picture'. This helps develop understanding that they are not just learning a range of different mathematics concepts and skills in insolation.

This chapter focuses on the connections beyond the subject of mathematics, exploring how links can be made to mathematics across the Early Years Foundation Stage (EYFS) and to other aspects of children's daily lives. This encourages children to see the application of maths to all their activities and the world around them, appreciating that it is an integral and integrated part of daily life rather than a separate entity.

KEY IDEAS

Hansen and Vaukins (2011, p. 6) ascertain that 'many adults and children hold the perception that mathematics is often something that is "done", rather than something that is used everyday as part of our lives and are often unaware of how they use mathematical skills in their everyday tasks.'

ACTIVITY

Before going any further, take a few minutes to think about and jot down all the ways you have used maths so far today. (If you are reading this in the afternoon or evening perhaps just think about the last couple of hours!)

- Can you identify what aspects of maths were involved (for example, addition, fractions, percentages)?
- Can you identify what maths skills were involved (for example, measurement, estimation)?

We are assuming that your list for the above activity is quite an extensive one (even if it is still early in the morning!) Once we really start to consider all the maths involved in just making a cup of tea, a trip to the shops or our journey to work/school, we begin to appreciate how integrated it is into all we do and how much of it is actually second nature to us. To avoid the situation, Hansen and Vaukins (2011) describe our skill as educators is to draw these mathematical moments to the attention of the children we work with, alongside recognising and highlighting mathematical connections across the EYFS. This is perhaps even more important as US research found maths anxiety can be observed in children as early as in the first and second grade, and there is a correlation between anxiety and outcomes (Beilock and Willingham, 2014). Dawker, Sarkar and Looi (2016) explain 'one possible reason for the negative association between mathematics anxiety and actual performance is that people who have higher levels of math anxiety are more likely to avoid activities and situations that involve mathematics.' This understandably could create a cycle as the maths avoidance impacts on learning and practice which in turn increases the anxiety. As this anxiety is observed when children begin their schooling, it is important to note that, as Beilock and Willingham (2014) explain, there is some evidence that children discern from parents, peers and teachers that maths is a subject to be anxious about, and those who begin school with 'deficiencies in basic mathematical skills' (p. 31) may be more likely to identify social cues that present maths in a negative way. Therefore, rather than maths being seen as a separate entity, as perhaps one to be feared, being aware of the role maths plays in everyday life and the world around them will be beneficial for all children in their early experiences and education, helping them see and appreciate their natural, daily relationship with the subject.

With so many everyday situations available to explore mathematically, it really seems unnecessary to have to create tenuous links or contrived contexts for mathematics learning. One of our favourite summaries of this situation is from Sally Brown, Charlie Brown's little sister, who states:

> *Only in math problems can you buy 60 cantaloupes*
>
> *and no one asks you what the heck is wrong with you.*

While we have so far identified aspects of daily routines, it is important to remember that everyday situations and contexts for children are not just these occurrences. Fairy tales, story books, block play, den making... these are all the very real daily tasks children engage with that also provide opportunities for meaningful mathematical learning opportunities.

Alongside the idea that maths is something that is 'done', it is also important to recognise that mathematics is often treated as a subject in isolation. Perhaps due to its perceived numerical nature or because it is viewed as a discrete set of skills and content, on topic-based planning maths is often the outlier that is not integrated into the topic of 'castles and fairy tales' or 'all about me'. While the EYFS acknowledges that 'all areas of learning and development are important and interconnected' (DfE, 2021, p. 7) the overview of mathematics is more targeted as it discusses the importance of 'developing a strong grounding in number... so that all children develop the building blocks to excel mathematically' (ibid, p. 10). The Primary National Curriculum (DfE, 2013, p. 9) goes on to be more specific as it highlights the expected integration of mathematics into all areas of the curriculum, stating:

- Teachers should use every relevant subject to develop pupils' mathematical fluency. Confidence in numeracy and other mathematical skills is a precondition of success across the National Curriculum.

- Teachers should develop pupils' numeracy and mathematical reasoning in all subjects so that they understand and appreciate the importance of mathematics.

The importance of integrating maths across all aspects of play and learning is highlighted by Bryce-Clegg (2017), who notes that specific maths areas, without adult presence, are not usually used by children for engaging with mathematics. Instead, it is in the continuous provision, when enhanced by mathematics resources, that children are engaging with practical maths experiences. The Education Endowment Foundation (EEF) guidance report (2020, p. 19) also promotes these ideas for Early Years and Key Stage 1 environments, stating, 'practitioners can provide extra opportunities to explore mathematics by highlighting where mathematics exists elsewhere in the curriculum. However, practitioners should carefully consider how to embed purposeful mathematical learning opportunities at an appropriately challenging level.'

ACTIVITY

Consider the other six areas of learning and development outlined in the EYFS framework ('Communication and Language', 'Personal, Social and Emotional Development', 'Physical Development', 'Literacy', 'Understanding the World' and 'Expressive Arts and Design').

- Which areas to you feel offer the most potential for the real and purposeful use of mathematics?
- Are there any areas for which you are struggling to find links to mathematics?

As you approach your planning for mathematics take some time to consider which of the other areas for learning there might be connections too. Similarly, are there any daily activities (such as registration, snack time, tidying up etc.) that involve the maths you are going to be teaching? If so, consider ways in which you might be able to use those connections as a context for learning, to show children the purpose of the mathematics they are learning and how it will underpin other aspects of their daily lives.

While some of these areas may instinctively appear to have more mathematical links, in the same way that most elements of our daily lives as adults are underpinned by mathematics, connections can be made across all the areas of the EYFS. For the first activity of the chapter, we asked you to identify the aspects of maths and the maths skills involved in your daily activities. As we consider the maths connections in the EYFS, it is helpful to consider these in the broader contexts of 'spatial reasoning', 'pattern and connection' and 'number'.

REFLECTION

- Can you categorise the maths in your daily activities more broadly as either involving 'spatial reasoning', 'pattern and connection', 'number' or a combination of these?
- Does this broader categorisation help you consider further links between mathematics and other areas of the EYFS framework?

We recommend that when you are planning any learning opportunity, you consider whether there are any connections that can be made to mathematics, either explicitly or by the provision in the environment. Before exploring some specific examples, we think it is helpful to identify some broad links to mathematics within each area of learning in the EYFS.

COMMUNICATION AND LANGUAGE

The EYFS framework states that 'the development of children's language underpins all seven areas of learning and development' (DfE, 2021, p. 8). When considering how much of children's play and daily interactions involve mathematics, the idea that 'by commentating on what children are interested in or doing and echoing back what they say with new vocabulary added, practitioners will build children's language effectively' is a key one for developing the use and accuracy of mathematical terms. How we can do this sensitively and effectively is discussed in Chapter 6: How are we talking?

Through its underpinning nature, mathematics will appear in all the other EYFS areas and many aspects of children's play. Actively looking for opportunities to use accurate and specifically chosen mathematical vocabulary (as discussed both Chapters 3 and 6) will help build children's confidence so they become comfortable using the 'rich range of vocabulary and language structures' (ibid) that underpins mathematics. This will also develop their confidence to share their mathematical ideas and have the vocabulary to discuss their thinking and reasoning.

PERSONAL, SOCIAL AND EMOTIONAL DEVELOPMENT

While some aspects of this area do have direct mathematical links (such as children learning how to eat healthily and look after their bodies), a key aspect of this will be in helping promote children developing 'a positive sense of self' and having 'confidence in their own abilities' (DfE, 2020, p. 9). As discussed in Chapter 3, people tend to develop very different relationships with mathematics, so ensuring we promote positive relationships with mathematics from early experiences is essential. This is particularly important if you do feel you have a negative relationship with mathematics, as research suggests maths anxiety can be transmitted from teachers to learners with implications for outcomes, and with the gender specific implication that girls are more likely to be affected by female teachers showing maths anxiety (Beilock & Willingham, 2014). Maths anxiety will cause children to experience negative emotions and a negative sense of self – exactly the opposite of that we are trying to promote.

A key message of this area for learning is the importance of adult support, modelling and guidance. As role models, we need to be promoting a positive message about mathematics and showing our enthusiasm for the subject. We need to model a positive attitude to learning, while actively making sure we are not reiterating any stereotypes such as maths being a boys' subject or the idea of 'not being a maths person'. Showcasing resilience is also essential, supporting children to 'set themselves simple goals' (DfE, 2020, p. 9) and persist in achieving these, enabling them to have and celebrate the successes in their early mathematical learning.

PHYSICAL DEVELOPMENT

The physical development overview in the EYFS framework highlights how 'by creating games and providing opportunities for play both indoors and outdoors, adults can support children to develop their core strength, stability, balance, spatial awareness, coordination and agility... Repeated and varied opportunities to explore and play with small world activities, puzzles, arts and crafts and the practice of using small tools, with feedback and support from adults, allow children to develop proficiency, control and confidence' (DfE, 2021, p. 9). Here, we see the core idea of developing spatial awareness running through the framework. As such, providing these varied opportunities is going to have an impact on both children's physical development and their spatial awareness, with all the mathematical benefits of this that are described in Chapter 3. Linking this to the idea of communication and language, as adults, if we are describing the activities using specific mathematical vocabulary and giving feedback on the mathematical elements of the spatial awareness alongside the physical development feedback, this is a simple and effective way of making important connections to mathematics in this area of children's learning and development.

Alongside the development of motor skills, there are also opportunities to develop mathematical thinking through PE and practice-related number skills. Tying in with the literacy focus below, *Spinderella* by Julia Donaldson (2016) is a lovely book to highlight the relevance of mathematics (number in particular) in creating fair teams and keeping score in sports. There is also an opportunity to develop initial understanding of counting in multiples when exploring how much of each bit of football kit is needed. When participating in sports activities themselves, as children practise specific skills, they can keep count of successful attempts in order to try and achieve personal bests.

LITERACY

There is perhaps a tendency to polarise mathematics and literacy, one as a creative subject and one as a practical and factual subject (but we hope by now we have dispelled these beliefs about maths!) However, there are some clear and important links between the two subjects.

As a very practical link to literacy, Saj and Barisnikov (2015) explain spatial perception underpins our ability to read. As children learn to read and write, they need to make sense of the shapes of letters, how these are combined to form words and the use of marks and spaces between them. They also need to learn which way to read across a page and how the structures of a book lead the way through the text. Interestingly Clements and Samara (2016, p. 86) explain early maths knowledge 'also predicts later reading achievement – even better than early literacy skills do'.

Alongside the practicalities, there are also many wonderful opportunities to explore mathematics through stories, an approach the EEF (2020) explains can be particularly effective. Story telling not only brings mathematical concepts to life, it creates memorable experiences and has the additional benefit of developing children's mathematical ability as stories enhance logical and analytical thinking (Pound & Lee, 2022). While we can all think of our favourite stories with mathematical themes, there are many lists available through simple searches that offer lots of ideas. Both 'DREME' (Development and Research in Early Math Education) and 'Maths Through Stories' have a wide variety of recommendations, including mapped to specific concepts/skills that may be the focus of learning. The links to these websites are in the 'Further Reading/Resources' section of this chapter.

UNDERSTANDING THE WORLD

It is very difficult to summarise the mathematical connections that can be found in the expectations of the 'understanding the world' aspect of the EYFS! If you have not yet watched Eddie Woo's TED Talk (recommended in Chapter 2), this is a fantastic starting point for considering how we view the world around us and develop a feeling for the maths hidden in plain sight. Pound and Lee (2022, p. 155) reiterate these ideas, explaining, 'the outdoors provides us with the space and many opportunities to teach mathematics in creative and enriching ways. By not only taking mathematics outside but also acknowledging the wonderful world of mathematics to be found in the natural world and in constructed buildings and artefacts, we encourage children to see mathematics as relevant to them and their interests and understandings.'

As the EYFS framework statement identifies various experiences for children outside the usual learning environment, such as visiting parks, libraries and museums (DfE, 2021, p. 10), it is helpful for us to consider what mathematical connections (such as mapping which develops spatial reasoning) can be identified and plan ways to build these into the visits.

EXPRESSIVE ARTS AND DESIGN

Pattern is a key idea as we develop both children's appreciation of expressive arts and design, and their understanding of what mathematics is all about. We ascertain that pattern is at the heart of mathematics and Pound and Lee (2022, p. 129) suggest 'music and dance are undoubtably the "art of pattern"'. Both music and dance offer children many ways to express patterns, and opportunities can be created to develop representation for these expressions. Additionally, in the same way that stories are memorable, songs, rhythm and rhymes can be used to help support children's developing memory of mathematical facts. Pound and Lee (2022) highlight the communal learning benefits of this approach alongside the enjoyment, motivation and opportunities for supporting physical actions this can involve.

There are also many amazing and inspiring opportunities to introduce children to art and architecture that have mathematics at their heart, supporting the intension of developing 'children's artistic and cultural awareness' (DfE, 2021, p. 10). For example, exploring ideas such as tessellation through tiling patterns or mosaics or the intricate geometric patterns in Islamic art, children can actively engage in developing their own artwork inspired by these. This will give children an opportunity to explore shapes and their properties in a meaningful way. Children can create patterns using a wide range of materials and experiences, all the while developing their ability to describe and reflect on their patterns, refining their understanding of the mathematical structures of these, be they repeating patterns, growth patterns or symmetrical patterns.

UNIQUE CHILD

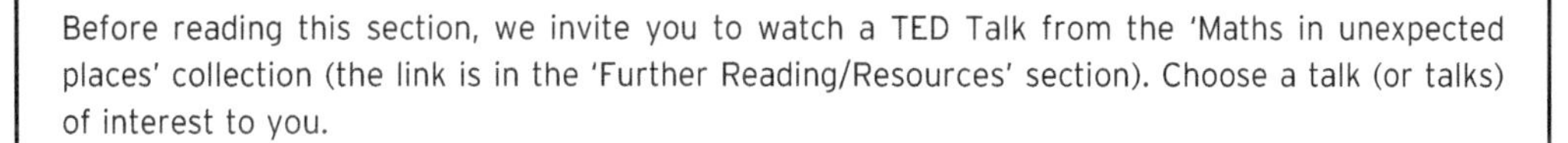

ACTIVITY

Before reading this section, we invite you to watch a TED Talk from the 'Maths in unexpected places' collection (the link is in the 'Further Reading/Resources' section). Choose a talk (or talks) of interest to you.

The talk you chose is likely to have been inspired by your current interests, or by something that caught your eye as something you have questions about or would like to find out more about. If you are anything like us, after having watched one of those talks, or listened to an interesting mathematical podcast, the key ideas just seem to naturally ebb out into our conversations. We have lost track of the times we end up using phrases such as, 'Oh, let me just tell you about this interesting thing I heard...' (perhaps to the amused smiles and slight eye rolling of our friends and colleagues!) However, our excitement is a little contagious and ultimately the other person's interest is usually piqued!

It goes without saying that the children in our classes are all individuals with individual interests. They want to tell you about the things that interest them (how the Flying Scotsman got its number, why they prefer street dance class to ballet, how many lengths they swam at the weekend, why Captain America is actually the best Marvel character...) Inevitably, there are going to be opportunities to explore maths in all these areas of interest and perhaps opportunities to use these areas of interest as stimulus for whole class or group learning.

CASE STUDY

Take Coralie for example. Coralie has an almost encyclopaedic knowledge of dinosaurs. She loves to talk about them and much prefers the realistic representations than 'friendly looking toys'. One thing that Coralie loves to do is sort her dinosaurs.

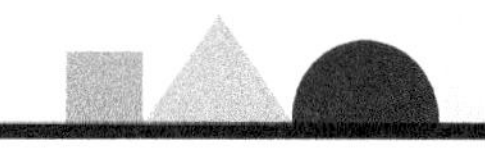

REFLECTION

As Coralie's teacher, how could you use her interest to develop her mathematical understanding? What sorting criteria might you encourage Coralie to use? How might she be encouraged to record her sorting?

Coralie might be encouraged to sort her dinosaurs according to size. When supporting Coralie to do this, we would need to think carefully about what aspect of 'size' is going to measured. As discussed in Chapter 3, we would want to avoid ambiguous vocabulary such as 'big'. Is it going to be the height of the dinosaurs, or will it be the length? Where would this be measured from and to? Does Coralie understand that these are in fact both measures of length? Coralie is likely to be engaged in direct comparison at this point, so how do we encourage her to develop key measurement skills such as using the same starting point?

Alternatively, Coralie might be wanting to group her dinosaurs in some other way, for example, those with horns, those with wings etc. We might encourage Coralie to use sorting circles to do this. However, what happens when Coralie finds a dinosaur that fits into both categories? Creating the overlap in the sorting circles will support her developing understanding of sorting criteria and ultimately Venn diagrams. Coralie may choose to draw this representation of her sorting, but equally she may choose to use a tally chart style to record her groupings, especially if they are distinct, rather than overlapping categories. Importantly, Coralie has now been exposed to a variety of ways of sorting the dinosaurs and of recording these. This could lead into conversations about the most effective way of representing her work to share with others, a key aspect of effective use of statistics and data visualisations as we progress through the statistics curriculum in later years.

POSITIVE RELATIONSHIPS

Again, it goes without saying that for children to want to seek you out and talk to you about their interests, you will need to have formed positive relationships with them. This may involve hearing about the different types of dinosaurs in great detail and perhaps even reading up about these yourself so you can ask knowledgeable questions to show Coralie you are interested in what she has told you. If Coralie feels you have a genuine interest in dinosaurs, she is far more likely to be receptive to your ideas and suggestions.

While quite naturally there will be some of the children's interests that you find more interesting than others, taking the time to genuinely listen to each child, ask questions and develop your understanding of their interests will enable you to engage with them in a deeper way. If you take this time to show your respect for them, they will trust your interest and motivations when you do draw out mathematical connections, rather than seeing you as shoe-horning your own agenda into their time (discussed further in Chapter 8).

Like the discussion in Chapter 4, knowing your children will also help you understand when to use a child's interest as a stimulus for a whole class piece of learning, and when not too. Some children will thrive on the fact that their interest is shared with the whole class and will happily talk about it to set the scene. Some children will be shy but appreciate the nudge and their confidence will grow as they are talking about something that they are passionate about. However, for some children this would not be helpful, so knowing your children well is going to be essential.

Another factor to consider in order to develop positive relationships is showing the children that they have a voice within the class and the wider school community that is valued. Consider the benefits of allowing children to vote on some class decisions or ensuring you have Early Years representation on your school council or eco council. Through this, children will be involved in decision-making, perhaps developing an understanding of the mathematics behind different decisions (such as the benefits of introducing crisp packet recycling bins or how much money different options for charity events might raise). This will not only help children understand the mathematical thinking process behind making many decisions but also introduce an initial, contextual understanding of statistical thinking.

ENABLING ENVIRONMENTS

ACTIVITY

Have a look at the images below. Jot down the first questions that come to mind (Figures 7.1–7.3).

Figure 7.1

(Continued)

(Continued)

Figure 7.2

Figure 7.3

Consider how many (if any!) of your questions had underlying elements of mathematics to them. Mathematical thinking is not an alien or abstract concept to children, so it is important we give them opportunities to verbalise their thoughts and develop their mathematical thinking. Providing interesting pictures as a stimulus is an interesting way to start mathematical conversations and something that could be done at different points throughout the day. It could take the form of a pre-assembly time-filler activity, a snack-time conversation, a picture of the week or part of a guided maths activity. Be on the lookout for interesting pictures and keep a folder of these (either digital or printed) as a useful resource.

Photographs could also be used to form a maths trail for the children to follow and explore. Maths trails can be used as children explore different environments or go on local visits and trips that are planned. A maths trail is an opportunity to explore meaningful connections and the scope is endless! Trails could be tailored to a particular mathematical topic or could explore a variety of maths topics that are encompassed within a place or environment. Again, it is essential to ensure the maths explored is real and purposeful, while minimising tenuous links, contrived situations and the arbitrary use of mathematics. Key questions you might want to ask yourself when planning a maths trial include:

- Is there a particular focus of the trail?
- Are the children being challenged?
- Will the trail improve the children's mathematical thinking?
- Does the trail support the expectations of the EYFS?
- Is the trail underpinned by what you consider to be good maths teaching (for example, are there opportunities to talk or for children to visualise the maths involved?)

Two Nrich articles are offered as further reading for this topic, one of which gives examples of meaningful maths trails which could be used as inspiration for developing your own trails.

The outdoor learning environment is an essential part of an enabling environment and offers many opportunities to explore maths and mathematical thinking. Learning Through Landscapes is a charity 'dedicated to enhancing outdoor learning and play for children' that offers suggestions for activities and stimuli.

ACTIVITY

Have a look at the activity suggestions for mathematics from Learning Through Landscapes (the link is in the 'Further Reading/Resources' section).

- How could you envisage adapting any of the activities for use in your teaching?
- Would they be guided activities or could they be independent?
- Would they be maths specific activities or incorporated as part of another area of your provision?

As you consider learning outside the classroom, think about the different opportunities that the changes in seasons may offer (for example, exploring pattern through snowflakes in winter or growing seeds in spring). Similarly, as you plan for different events in the academic calendar (such as school fairs or sports day), explore the mathematics potential of these. Incorporating maths into these aspects and sharing this with the children will further increase their awareness of the integrated nature of mathematics to the world around them.

SUMMARY

Pound and Lee (2022, p. 108) explain:

> *Children learn mathematical (and other) skills best at the time when they need to use them in meaningful, relevant and real contexts. Mathematics teaching and learning being based on cross-curricular activity creates opportunities to set mathematical ideas and concepts in an environment where they have real purpose, relevance and meaning. If mathematics is placed in the context of other areas of learning, children's understanding is enriched, challenged and affirmed.*

As you plan for learning across all areas of the EYFS framework, take a moment to consider what connections to mathematics could be developed; also consider what you know of the children in your class, their interests, hobbies and daily activities and what maths is involved in these that you could highlight and explore. As you develop these connections, take time to ensure you are focusing on meaningful, mathematical learning opportunities that minimise tenuous links, contrived situations and the arbitrary use of mathematics. Instead, look for all opportunities to maximise the real and purposeful use of mathematics.

FURTHER READING/RESOURCES

Crack, A. (2011 revised 2022). *Meaningful maths trails*. Nrich. https://nrich.maths.org/2579

DREME: 40 Children's books that foster a love of math. https://dreme.stanford.edu/news/children-s-books-foster-love-math

Learning through landscapes: Outdoor lesson ideas. https://www.ltl.org.uk/free-resources/?swoof=1&pa_subject=mathematics

Maths through stories. https://www.mathsthroughstories.org/

Piggott, J., & Pumfrey, L. (2011). *Maths trails*. Nrich. https://nrich.maths.org/5456

Pound, L., & Lee, T. (2022). *Teaching mathematics creatively* (3rd ed.). London: Routledge. Chapter 6: Once upon a time: Using story to learn and teach maths.

TED: Maths in unexpected places. https://www.ted.com/playlists/401/math_in_unexpected_places

REFERENCES

Beilock, S., & Willingham, D. T. (2014). Ask the cognitive scientist: Maths anxiety: Can teachers help students reduce it? *American Educator, 38*(2), 28–32.

Bryce-Clegg, A. (2017). *Effective transition into year 1*. London: Featherstone Education.

Clements, D. H., & Samara, J. (2016). Math, science, and technology in the early grades. *Future of Children, 26*(2), 75–94.

Dawker, A., Sarker, A., & Looi, C. Y. (2016). Mathematics anxiety: What have we learned in 60 years? *Frontiers in Psychology, 7*, 508.

DfE. (2013). *The national curriculum in England: Key stages 1 and 2 framework document*. https://assets.publishing.service.gov.uk/government/uploads/system/uploads/attachment_data/file/425601/PRIMARY_national_curriculum.pdf

DfE. (2021). *Statutory framework for the early years foundation stage*. https://assets.publishing.service.gov.uk/government/uploads/system/uploads/attachment_data/file/974907/EYFS_framework_-_March_2021.pdf

DonaldsonJ. (2016). *Spinderella* (S. Braun, Illus.) London: Egmot UK Limited.

Education Endowment Foundation. (2020). *Improving Mathematics in the Early Years and Key Stage 1*. https://educationendowmentfoundation.org.uk/education-evidence/guidance-reports/early-maths

Hansen, A., & Vaukins, D. (2011). *Primary mathematics across the curriculum*. London: SAGE Learning Matters.

Pound, L., & Lee, T. (2022). *Teaching mathematics creatively* (3rd ed.). London: Routledge.

Saj, A., & Barisnikov, K. (2015). Influence of spatial perception abilities on reading in school-age children. *Cogent Psychology*, *2*(1), 10.

8

IS IT PURPOSEFUL. . . AND WHAT IF. . .?

CHAPTER OBJECTIVES

- Consolidate ideas about what makes mathematical learning purposeful
- Explore how to respond to unexpected situations

INTRODUCTION

Two key aspects of planning and practice are explored in this chapter. Firstly, we consolidate ideas explored in previous chapters, considering the purpose of the mathematics that is occurring in our classroom and importantly who it is purposeful for. We then go on to consider the '. . . but what if. . .' moments that will invariably occur as we are working in education! It can be the thought of these moments that create feelings of nervousness or anxiety when planning for any mathematical learning opportunity, especially if you do not feel you are confident with your own mathematical knowledge. In this chapter we will explore an underpinning model for these occasions and create a checklist of suggestions for what to do if you find yourself taken by surprise.

This chapter follows a slightly different structure to the previous chapters, as we do not explicitly consider the unique child, positive relationships or the learning environment, but these are woven in throughout the exploration of the key ideas.

KEY IDEAS

IS IT PURPOSEFUL? WHO IS IT PURPOSEFUL FOR?

Alf Coles (2021) begins his TEDx talk by explaining he has spent his teaching career 'puzzling the question of how learning mathematics can become relevant to students' lives, connected to things that they care about and significant for the world that we live in.' This question is key if we are to encourage children to see mathematics as purposeful. We have already considered in Chapters 2 and 3, how the way we see the world might influence what we draw out to be purposeful in mathematics and how this might then influence how and what we teach; what we draw the children's attention to and what we perhaps skim over or overlook. Through Chapters 4 to 6, many facets of purpose have been identified and addressed, carefully considering our purpose as we plan opportunities for play, talk and exploring mathematical concepts using manipulatives and images. Chapter 7 highlights the many ways in which maths is connected to our everyday lives and other aspects of the EYFS statutory framework, revealing many inherent purposeful links. So, the key question for this chapter, in relation to planning mathematical learning opportunities, is, 'who is it purposeful for?'

For children, purposeful opportunities for engaging with mathematics are going to arise naturally through their play. Through this engagement, opportunities can be identified as teachable moments or incorporated into future guided learning opportunities. If you are playing and spot an opportunity for a teachable moment, who is that opportunity important for? At that moment, is it going to enhance the children's play? Will they be open to it as an opportunity to enhance their learning and understanding, or will it just interfere with the flow of their play, their thought process and as a result create a potential barrier to their level of engagement with you and what you are proposing they think about? As the adult, are you putting your agenda for children's learning above what is naturally occurring? Fisher (2016, p. 43) explains that 'when a practitioner has an objective in mind, then it is harder to find space for the objectives of the child'.

Throughout the other chapters we have discussed the importance of getting the balance right in terms of acting on teachable moments. Malaguzzi (1994), founder of the Reggio Emilia Approach, explains the need to initiate situations where children learn by themselves, with autonomy and as little adult intervention as possible. He states, 'We don't want to teach children something that they can learn by themselves. We don't want to give them thoughts that they can come up with by themselves. What we want to do is activate within children the desire and will and great pleasure that comes from being the authors of their own learning.' Fisher (2016, p. 3) explains that the work of the Oxfordshire Adult-Child Interaction Project identified the following criteria being used to assess whether interactions between adults and children were effective:

- Learning has to be enhanced
- The interaction has to be enhanced by the practitioner
- The child's experience must be positive

It can be helpful to use these three criteria to help determine whether we feel it is appropriate to engage in a teachable moment during children's play or when to let the moment pass but make a note of the observation to incorporate at another time.

REFLECTION

Do you feel more emphasis should be placed on the teaching and learning of number as it is the focus of the Early Learning Goals? How much focus should be placed on developing spatial reasoning and pattern?

When considering guided learning opportunities in particular, we know that there are certain things children are expected to know by the time they finish their Reception year. These expectations are presented as the Early Learning Goals and in mathematics have a focus on number (DfE, 2021). As a teacher, we will probably consider an essential part of the purpose of our teaching to be children having met these expectations. However, Fisher (2016, p. 43) explains 'the increased emphasis in recent years on outcomes (be they welfare requirements or educational goals) has created tension for all Early Years practitioners as they attempt to achieve the targets set by adults, rather than those preferred by children.' This has important implications for practice as it can create a perceived hierarchy in learning early mathematics, where the role of number is valued more than developing spatial reasoning or exploring pattern and connections. This can lead to a situation where all guided learning opportunities focus on number, while engagement with shape and measures are only part of free play or enhanced provision. However, as discussed in Chapter 3, it is clear that work on developing spatial reasoning and developing pattern and connection underpins early conceptual understanding of many aspects of number. As such, if as educators we see the purpose of teaching and learning to be to meet specified outcomes, there is a danger that teaching becomes focused on reaching these end goals, rather than developing the richer tapestry of connections and conceptual understanding that is needed to underpin this learning.

ACTIVITY

Explore the Early Years 'measures', 'shape and space' and 'pattern' activity suggestions from Nrich (the link is in the 'Further Reading/Resources' section). As you do, consider:

1. The purpose of engaging with these activities as part of developing children's holistic conceptual understanding in mathematics;
2. How the activities might be purposefully integrated into your classroom practices, routines and play.

At this point, we would like to introduce a potential framework that you might find helpful to guide your thinking as you plan opportunities to explore mathematics (Figure 8.1).

While the intended activity sits at the centre of the guided learning, it is informed and enhanced by the key themes of play, representation, talk, purpose and connections.

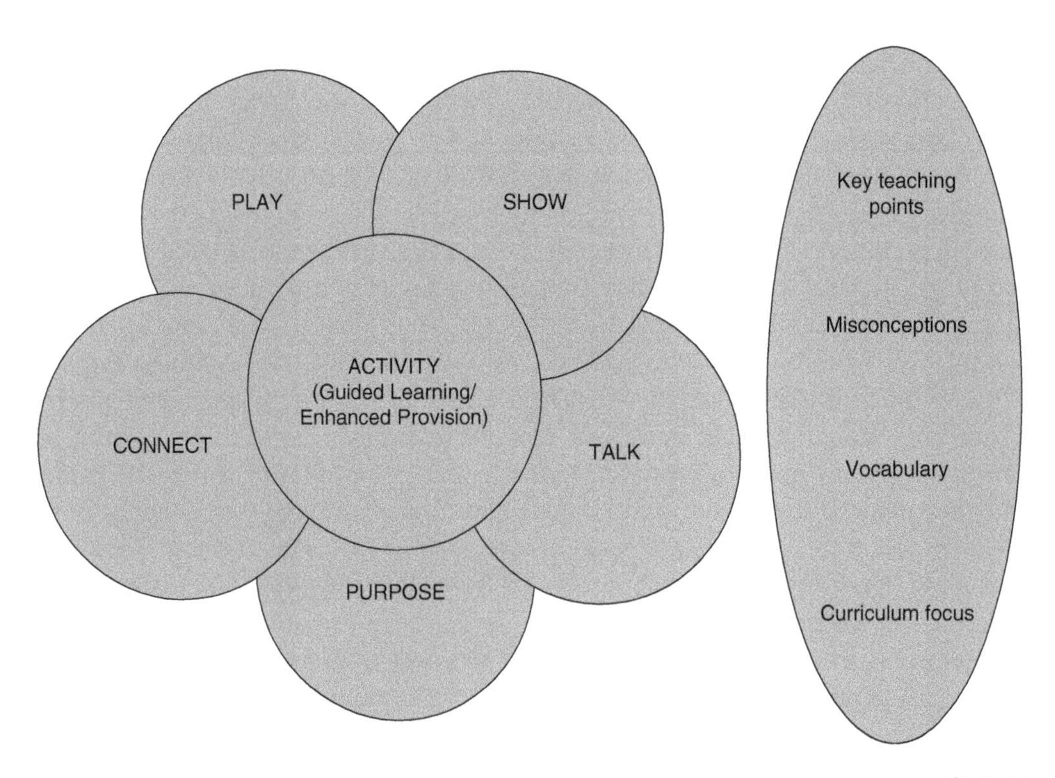

Figure 8.1

Enhanced provision opportunities can also be developed in relation to the guided learning, considering how these build on and complement each other. The opportunity to specify the key teaching points, potential misconceptions, specific vocabulary choices and curriculum focus, not only ensures appropriate coverage, but we find also increases confidence to teach, as these key aspects have been carefully considered in advance. We always advocate reading to inform practice, so we have included some suggestions for further reading you could use to identify key teaching points, potential misconceptions and key vocabulary for the maths you are teaching. Chapter 3 also covers many of these key ideas for different aspects of early mathematics.

'. . .WHAT IF. . .?'

Periodically, around exam time, there always seems to be a lovely set of funny exam answers that do the rounds showcasing children's (often) well-considered but unexpected answers. We have a giggle at them, admire the lateral thinking and, as educators, perhaps we spend just a couple of moments reflecting on why they have given that answer. This section of the chapter draws on that type of reflection, when we get the unexpected answers to our questions, and how we can deal with these situations in a meaningful way.

This type of planning fits into the final category of Rowland et al.'s (2009) Knowledge Quartet and by its nature does not really fit on a planning proforma (although we can prepare for common potential misconceptions). Rowland et al. (2009) categorise this as 'contingency' knowledge and it has three associated codes: deviation from the agenda, responding to children's ideas and use of opportunities. We have already considered use of opportunities in the previous chapter, so in this chapter we focus on how and when we might deviate from our agenda (our plan) and how and when we might respond to the children's ideas.

ACTIVITY

Can you write down a definition of contingency for a classroom context?

Rowland et al. (2009, p. 126) explain, '[Contingency] is all about in-the-moment actions and interactions in the classroom and the unpredictability of these actions. Teachers are continually responding to the interests and understandings of children as part of their engagement with the children's learning. However, because it is impossible to know how each individual will react and respond to any situation, teachers have to be ready to make decisions "on their feet" during the course of the lesson.'

We are sure that on a day-to-day basis you will find plenty of examples of situations that fit this definition! Once you tune into key ideas such as the language the teacher is using, sometimes these situations can easily be demystified. Take for example the children that started a very enthusiastic conversation about the last time they had a McDonald's (other fast-food outlets are available!) in a lesson about subtraction. Much as the teacher was initially a little taken aback, she soon realised they were all using the language of 'take away' in these discussions. After taking a moment to reconsider her choice of vocabulary and explain to the children the difference between the everyday use of the term 'take away' and the mathematical version related to the model for subtraction, the learning was back on track.

Rowland et al. (2009, p. 50) explain that these moments may arise from specific stimuli:

- a child's response to a question from the teacher;
- a child's response to an activity or discussion;
- a child's incorrect answer to a question or in the course of a discussion.

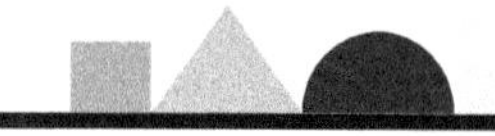

REFLECTION

Can you think of any times when you have been taken by surprise by a child's response in any of these situations? How did you respond to the child? Did your response have a positive or negative effect on the situation?

From their observations of teaching, Rowland et al. (2009, p. 133) identified three common ways in which teachers respond to unexpected situations:

1. ignore the situation;
2. acknowledge the situation but side line it;
3. respond to the situation and incorporate it.

Considering your responses to the reflection opportunity, do you think you responded to the situation in one of the ways proposed above? The choice to respond in one of these ways will probably be connected to both the purpose of your intended teaching/learning opportunity and your level of confidence with what you are teaching. What follows are some case studies to exemplify these ideas and consider the effect the choice of response might have on teaching and learning.

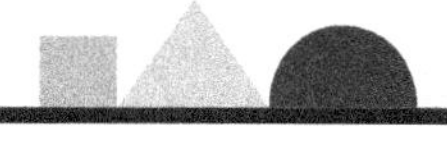

(1) CASE STUDY: IGNORING THE SITUATION

An Early Years colleague came into the staff room a little flustered during morning break time. When asked what was wrong, they replied that they had just been teaching odd and even numbers and one of the children in their Reception class had called out to ask, 'Is infinity an odd or an even number?' The colleague admitted to being so thrown by the question, and the fact they did not know the answer, that they just pretended they had not heard and moved on.

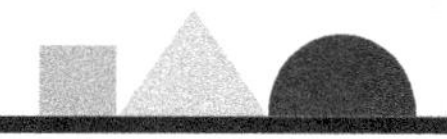

REFLECTION

How do you think you would have responded in that situation? How do you think the colleague feels about the way they responded? What effect do you think that response had on the child who asked the question?

An important message at this point is that it is okay not to know the answer to a question. What is important is how we respond to these questions. By ignoring a situation children may develop or maintain misconceptions (in this case that infinity is a quantifiable number) or they may come to believe that their input is not valid or appreciated, in which case they may stop asking these wonderful questions. If you find yourself in a situation where you do not know the answer, it is okay to say that and to compliment the child on asking such an interesting question. Depending on the question you may promise to look into it for the child or explore it with them, modelling good mathematical behaviours of enquiry. Some questions just require a quick internet search, such as when you are asked the name of an eleven-sided shape. Conducting this search with the child both models your commitment as a learner and gives the child confidence that what they might see as 'adult expertise' is not inherent, but something that is developed over time.

(2) CASE STUDY: ACKNOWLEDGE THE SITUATION BUT SIDE LINE IT

In an observation of a guided play intervention on number bonds to ten, as a plenary activity the group were working together to list all the number bond pairs they had found. The teacher was encouraging them to spot patterns within this by modelling working systematically. Having reached

(Continued)

(Continued)

what the teacher considered to be the conclusion of the activity, they asked the children two questions to encourage reasoning, 'Have we got them all? How do we know?' The teacher was surprised when Emily replied, 'No, you haven't got them all.' The teacher asked Emily to explain why she thought that, to which Emily replied, 'You haven't got minus ten and twenty, that makes ten'.

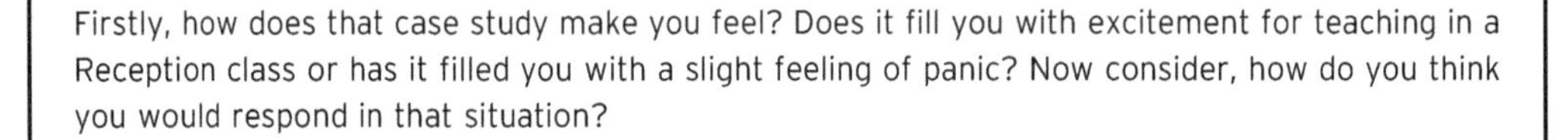

Firstly, how does that case study make you feel? Does it fill you with excitement for teaching in a Reception class or has it filled you with a slight feeling of panic? Now consider, how do you think you would respond in that situation?

This particular Early Years teacher enjoys teaching maths and is confident doing so, so the related subject-matter knowledge here did not unnerve them. In a follow up conversation, they explained they found the fact that this was being said to them by a just turned 5-year-old quite exciting! However, they made a decision in the moment to acknowledge but side line the situation. They thanked Emily for her answer and clarified that they had found all the answers using positive, whole numbers, which Emily agreed they had. However, they then went on to say to Emily that they were really interested in her answer and would like to explore it in more detail with her, so they would chat later in the day.

What is important in our context is the response of the teacher. By acknowledging the situation, Emily knew her input was valuable. However, the teacher recognised that continuing that conversion in front of the rest of the group went well beyond the scope of the intended learning and would likely cause confusion and potentially misconceptions. As such, they made the decision to have an individual conversation with Emily later in the day to assess her understanding or establish whether it was just a one off, random fact she knew.

When the teacher did catch up with Emily, they found that she had a secure understanding of negative numbers and could confidently calculate with them, crossing the zero boundary. What we are keen to point out here is that this an exceptional example but naturally this did have implications for planning for Emily in mathematics. Useful links were also established with her parents to help support and develop this. If you do find yourself in this situation and feel less confident than this teacher, remember that there are many other teachers in the setting or school who can support you. Talk to the maths lead for guidance and, as in this situation, make good links with the parents or carers.

(3) CASE STUDY: RESPOND TO THE SITUATION AND INCORPORATE IT

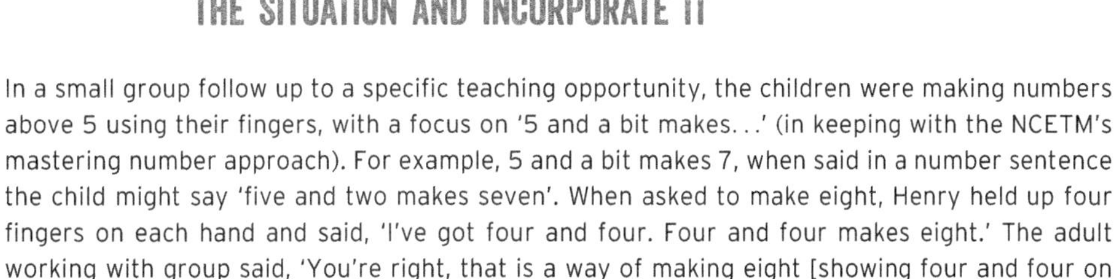

In a small group follow up to a specific teaching opportunity, the children were making numbers above 5 using their fingers, with a focus on '5 and a bit makes...' (in keeping with the NCETM's mastering number approach). For example, 5 and a bit makes 7, when said in a number sentence the child might say 'five and two makes seven'. When asked to make eight, Henry held up four fingers on each hand and said, 'I've got four and four. Four and four makes eight.' The adult working with group said, 'You're right, that is a way of making eight [showing four and four on her fingers], but we're thinking about five and a bit. What would you need to change to make this [holding up her fingers] five and a bit to make eight?' At this point, Henry held up his fingers again, looked down at his hands and carefully put down one finger on his right hand and lifted one finger up on his left hand. 'Now I've got five and three and it still makes eight,' he said.

We can see how the adult working with Henry acknowledged his contribution. It was positively met and through it the focus on '5 and a bit' was re-established. Through this simple interaction, Henry also has been given the opportunity (even though not explicit) to make patterns and connections about the different possible compositions of the number eight.

ACTIVITY

Have a look at the example below (Figure 8.2) that Eastaway and Askew (2010, p. 244) share. How would you respond to this child's answer?

This is an interesting situation as through their answer the child is showing their understanding of the concept of five. Eastaway and Askew (ibid) explain that 'this little girl liked cats, so she decided to adapt the question.' Here the given answer could easily be incorporated into the learning. Individually the answer could be discussed with the child, acknowledging their understating of the grouping of 5, and asking if they can see another group within the examples. The answer could also be shared, with the child's permission, with a wider group, who could explore why they had given this answer and whether they thought it was correct.

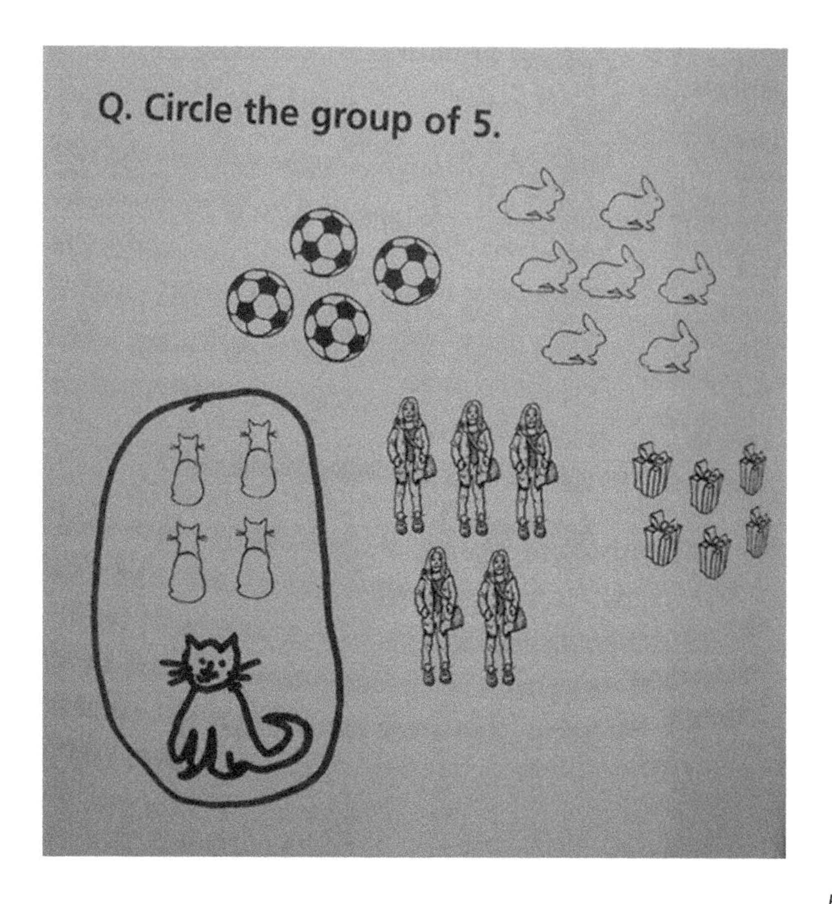

Figure 8.2

ACTIVITY

Having considered moments where unexpected situations may arise and Rowland et al.'s suggested responses, can you create a checklist, considering core principles for when you find yourself facing an unexpected situation?

By creating a checklist, you are not only giving yourself ideas to draw on, but you are also acknowledging that these situations will occur and hopefully developing your confidence to feel ready to respond to them. Rowland et al. (2009, p. 127) identify that an initial response from the teacher will probably be one that buys time while they consider possible responses, a pause and perhaps a question or statement such as 'That's an interesting thought' or 'Could you explain a little more?'. Some of the key ideas we would put on our own list would be to take a deep breath, have honest conversations (even if you find them a little daunting), let the children build the conversation, be a good listener, keep a neutral face, ask key probing questions, return to ideas later or in the next session, know where to go to find out if you are not sure... all these will help you build rapport and positive relationships with your learners, so you and they can explore mathematics together.

SUMMARY

Pound and Lee (2022) explain that while planning is essential to consider possible responses to activities and the mathematical learning that may arise, through capitalising on unexpected learning opportunities children's interests can be nurtured. Rowland et al.'s (2009, p. 126) explanation that, 'typically a teacher will be juggling several aspects... and often will have anticipated them. However, there are times when a teacher is faced with an unexpected response to a question or an unexpected point within a discussion and so has to make a decision whether or not to explore the idea with the child' succinctly summarises the key ideas from this chapter.

When planning for mathematical opportunities, it is essential we consider what the purpose of that opportunity is and who it is purposeful for. We need to be mindful of outcome agendas which may lead teaching to be directed for that purpose, rather than what we consider the overall purpose of learning mathematics to be. Through considering all the key themes of this book, meaningful purpose is likely to be established when planning. This planning can help ensure you feel more confident and also better prepared for the '...what if...' moments. Often these moments will be particularly purposeful for a child as they grapple with ideas and make connections, so it is essential we handle them sensitively and effectively. It is also important for us to embrace and enjoy these moments of unpredictability. As Malaguzzi (1994) explains:

> *School is not at all like billiards. When you play billiards you push the ball with a certain force and it hits the table and bounces off; there's a definite way the ball will go, depending on force and direction. Children are not at all like this, predictable. But sometimes schools function as if they were; these are schools with no joy.*

FURTHER READING/RESOURCES

Borthwick, A., Gifford, S., & Thouless, H. (2021). *The power of pattern – Patterning in the early years*. ATM.

Clements, D. H., & Sarama, J. (2017/2019). Learning and teaching with learning trajectories [LT]². https://www.learningtrajectories.org/math/learning-trajectories

Early Childhood Maths Group. (ECMG). https://earlymaths.org/

Haylock, D., & Cockburn, A. (2017). *Understanding mathematics for young children: A guide for teachers of children 3-7*. Los Angeles: SAGE.

NCETM: Early Years. https://www.ncetm.org.uk/in-the-classroom/early-years/

Nrich: Early Years Foundation Stage Activities. https://nrich.maths.org/13371

REFERENCES

Coles, A. (2021). *What we've got wrong about learning mathematics. TEDxBath what we've got wrong about learning mathematics*. Alf Coles, TEDxBath.

DfE. (2021). *Statutory framework for the early years foundation stage*. https://assets.publishing.service.gov.uk/government/uploads/system/uploads/attachment_data/file/974907/EYFS_framework_-_March_2021.pdf

Eastaway, R., & Askew, M. (2010). *Maths for mums and dads*. London: Square Peg.

Fisher, J. (2016). *Interacting or interfering?* Maidenhead: Open University Press.

Malaguzzi, L. (1994). *Your image of the child: Where teaching begins*. Childcare Information Exchange.

Pound, L., & Lee, T. (2022). *Teaching mathematics creatively* (3rd ed.). London: Routledge.

Rowland, T., Turner, F., Thwaites, A., & Huckstep, P. (2009). *Developing primary mathematics teaching*. London: SAGE Publications Ltd.

9

TRANSITION TO KEY STAGE ONE

CHAPTER OBJECTIVES

- Consider the ways in which effective Early Years practice in mathematics might continue into Key Stage 1.
- Develop knowledge of the Primary National Curriculum and how this can be worked with to ensure smooth transition from the Early Years Foundation Stage (EYFS).

INTRODUCTION

There are several key texts and resources that offer guidance on how best to establish Year 1 learning environments and the curriculum to support children's transition into Key Stage 1 (see 'Further Reading/Resources' at the end of this chapter), the key ideas of which we will summarise. In terms of a supportive transition in mathematics, we will also draw on our knowledge of the primary curriculum and common Key Stage 1 practice coupled with reference to the use of schemes of work and the effect of summative assessments on practice. The chapter concludes with recommendations for effective practice in strengthening mathematical foundations throughout Key Stage 1.

KEY IDEAS

As we have discussed throughout this book, the EYFS curriculum and related pedagogy emphasise child-centred mathematical learning in terms of topics and contexts that are of interest to each child and that develop from the knowledge, skills and understanding that they already hold. Many educators advocate for the continuation of this into Key Stage 1 (Bryce-Clegg, 2017; Early Years Matters, 2022; Fisher, 2020). However, it is also widely acknowledged that, historically, there has been a significant challenge when attempting this due to a non-alignment between the Early Learning Goals and the expectations of the Primary National Curriculum (Fisher, 2020; Ofsted, 2017). The 'new' EYFS and ELGs (DfE, 2021) were the result of attempts to re-align these, as discussed in the Introduction to Chapters 1–3. Despite this, many Year 1 teachers (similarly to many Reception teachers) grapple with a reality that the children they are teaching are 5–6 years old and for many, the transition to a more 'primary looking' classroom experience does not meet their developmental needs. Moving to Year 1, they argue, does not automatically mean that all children are ready to sit at desks and listen as part of a whole class for increasingly long periods of time, record their mathematical thinking in increasingly formal ways or follow a wholly adult initiated agenda for their maths learning. There is a concern, as raised by Early Years and primary mathematics specialists, that this leads to superficial compliance, reduced understanding, increased anxiety and increasingly insecure mathematical knowledge and skills. As a result, the transition to Key Stage 1 is preoccupied with the challenge of how and when to adapt provision; to what extent should Year 1 'look like' Reception, for how long; what is 'best practice' in Years 1 and 2, and why...?

REFLECTION

Reflect on the Year 1 mathematics practice you have seen. Does it differ from that in Early Years/Reception classes? In what ways? What impact have you seen transition have on children's learning? Conversely, do you think that Reception should 'look more like' Year 1? In what ways? What about Year 2?

The choices made about mathematical teaching and learning in Key Stage 1 can tell us a lot about the beliefs and assumptions held by teachers and senior leaders about what maths is, how children learn it and how it is best taught (as discussed in Chapters 2 and 3). Unpicking these, and the resulting tensions between differing viewpoints, is complex. Specific decisions in individual classrooms and schools are strongly dependent on context, but there are some choices that can be made that enable teachers of 5–7-year-olds to root their practice in what is best, or at the very least – not detrimental, to the children and the subject. It is also helpful to engage with what the statutory expectations and requirements for primary mathematics are, as documented in the Primary National Curriculum.

THE PRIMARY NATIONAL CURRICULUM: MATHEMATICS

We have already discussed some aspects of the Primary National Curriculum's 'Purpose of Study' statement (DfE, 2013) for mathematics in Chapter 2. However, it is worth acknowledging it in its entirety here:

> *Mathematics is a creative and highly inter-connected discipline that has been developed over centuries, providing the solution to some of history's most intriguing problems. It is essential to everyday life, critical to science, technology and engineering, and necessary for financial literacy and most forms of employment. A high-quality mathematics education therefore provides a foundation for understanding the world, the ability to reason mathematically, an appreciation of the beauty and power of mathematics, and a sense of enjoyment and curiosity about the subject. (p. 99)*

As you can see, 'creativity', 'inter-connectedness', 'beauty' and 'enjoyment' are embedded in the mathematics purpose of study statement and each of these ideas about what maths is and why we teach it run both explicitly and implicitly throughout this book.

The purpose of study is followed by an outline of three 'Aims' for mathematics teaching and learning as follows:

> *The National Curriculum for mathematics aims to ensure that all pupils:*
>
> - *become fluent in the fundamentals of mathematics, including through varied and frequent practice with increasingly complex problems over time, so that pupils develop conceptual understanding and the ability to recall and apply knowledge rapidly and accurately.*
> - *reason mathematically by following a line of enquiry, conjecturing relationships and generalisations, and developing an argument, justification or proof using mathematical language.*
> - *can solve problems by applying their mathematics to a variety of routine and non-routine problems with increasing sophistication, including breaking down problems into a series of simpler steps and persevering in seeking solutions.*
>
> (p. 99)

We can see that these explicitly reference conceptual understanding, variation, the ability to recall and apply knowledge, mathematical reasoning and spoken language, and perseverance in solving problems (DfE, 2013). Again, these ideas are fundamental to those that we have outlined throughout this book as core elements of effective practice in Early Years mathematics.

At a whole school level, there is an expectation that the programmes of study are taught by the end of their respective key stage and so, although they are also organised into distinct year groups, there is some flexibility and autonomy regarding when certain content is introduced. While, in line with the NCETM's mastery approach (Stripp, 2014), there is an expectation that all children will 'move through' the programmes of study at broadly the same pace, it is explicitly stated that a secure breadth and depth of understanding is an essential precursor to an acceleration through content (DfE, 2013). Those children who rapidly grasp key concepts and ideas should be offered further challenge through more sophisticated problems, while others are offered more opportunities to consolidate their understanding.

There is a strong and understandable temptation to meet this curriculum requirement by grouping children according to 'ability' which usually means 'prior attainment', and providing them with different tasks, starting points and/or resources. Increasingly, mathematics educators are voicing their concerns with this way of organising mathematical learning as it has the result of widening, rather than closing, any gaps in understanding or attainment in an unfair and limiting way (Boaler, 2022; Drury, 2014; Morgan, 2022). Such grouping might be overt in the form of group names or tables, or clearly labelled tasks or questions that children are directed towards; or covert in the form of conversations about 'highers' or 'lowers' at the point of planning or assumptions about who will or won't 'get' a new piece of learning that influence what is expected. Planning to use rich, open-ended tasks/problems/investigations with a whole class and using the pedagogical strategies we have outlined in Chapters 4–8 to interact with each child's responses is a powerful way to ensure that children continue to grow their understanding of 'big' mathematical goals within a supportive, democratic and inclusive environment. This approach also supports the National Curriculum in that while the programmes of study for each year group are 'by necessity, organised into apparently distinct domains ... pupils should make rich connections across mathematical ideas' (DfE, 2013, p. 99) and 'move fluently between representations of mathematical ideas' (ibid); again, these are ideas we have explored at length in Chapters 5 and 7.

SCHEMES OF WORK

The use of a scheme of work to support teachers to navigate the complexities of delivering the programmes of study has become increasingly prevalent in primary schools for Years 1 to 6 in England and Wales over the last decade. This has been strongly influenced by the adoption of the 'new' National Curriculum in 2014 and the coinciding growth in awareness of a 'mastery approach' to learning mathematics. Various 'schemes' are available to buy (e.g. Maths No Problem, Primary Stars, Power

Maths, Mathematics Mastery) or accessible for free via the NCETM (Addition and Subtraction, Multiplication and Division and Fractions 'Spines') or affiliated maths hub provision (White Rose Maths). There are differences between the materials provided, some cover the whole curriculum, some are focused on 'number', some have affiliated textbooks and/or workbooks, some have editable interactive whiteboard slides, some have teacher guides, but all of them provide a suggested teaching sequence across long-term, medium-term and short-term plans. These break down the National Curriculum programmes of study statements into smaller teaching steps with the intention that this will lead to the building up of children's mathematical knowledge, skills and understanding and enable them to show that they have met the age-related expectation for their year group by the end of the school year. Such 'schemes of work' offer a valuable supportive resource for schools by providing a baseline benchmark for primary teachers' mathematical subject-matter, pedagogical content and curriculum knowledge. It is perceived that use of a scheme reduces the risk that content could be 'missed', the potentially damaging effects of a teacher's lack of subject-matter or pedagogical knowledge, or that learning could be pitched inappropriately in relation to the curriculum goals.

However, the pressure to prioritise coverage of curriculum content to achieve these goals can influence a move away from a focus on playing and exploring, active learning, creative and critical thinking and a child-centred approach towards more formal pedagogy as children move into and through Key Stage 1 (Bryce-Clegg, 2017). The need to cover content and evidence progress and attainment as part of both internal and external accountability measures can lead teachers to favour the increasing atomisation of 'bits' of maths into linear sequences of small steps and necessitates endless compromises in meeting the needs of each unique child. To ensure all children can 'keep up', we see a bloating of mathematics teaching to include multiple models of adaptive teaching, pre-teaching, 'catch-ups', interventions, separate arithmetic/fluency sessions and lessons that can run to over an hour. Arguably, the extent to which this practice, which wholly prioritises the adult's agenda, can accommodate the characteristics of effective learning is limited.

Perhaps then, the non-alignment acknowledged at the start of this chapter is now not so clearly found in the comparison of the EYFS and Primary National Curriculum, but more in its interpretation according to educators' beliefs and assumptions, the pressure of evidencing progress and attainment, and the resulting *pedagogy* used to implement it.

The 'breaking down' of mathematics into small sequential steps fits well with Clements and Sarama's (in Maloney et al., 2014) work on mathematical learning trajectories. Learning trajectories are pathways of a suggested route that learners could take on the way to an increasingly sophisticated understanding of inter-related concepts or 'big ideas' in mathematics. They are not a simplistic 'checklist' of facts or skills that are to be attained but outline a progression in levels of thinking.

> *LTs' developmental progressions are more than linear sequences based on accretion of numerous facts and skills or a "progression" of assessment tasks...In this approach, effective instruction involves more than teaching a specific lesson or concept (such as "today we are focussing on counting objects") because such an approach does not account for levels of development, individual differences in children's abilities, or the connectedness of mathematical knowledge. Instead, instruction must also focus on the growth children experience in their progress towards the goal*
>
> (Clements et al., 2019, p. 2511)

Crucially, developing knowledge of mathematical learning trajectories (see 'Further Reading/Resources') could support teachers throughout Early Years/Reception and Key Stage 1 to better interpret what a child's actions, recordings and talk can tell us about their stage of mathematical learning and to respond in a way that prioritises their viewpoint (Sarama & Clements, 2009). Increasing teachers' knowledge of mathematical development, not as a list of tasks to be completed but as a progression in mathematical thinking behaviours, has the potential to increase both teacher and learner understanding and agency, and support mathematical interactions built on the richest of learning opportunities – a curious response to the interesting or unexpected.

Similarly, Fisher (2020) argues for a 'developmentally sensitive pedagogy' that continues into Key Stage 1, balances child-led, adult-led and adult-initiated learning, and must include play. As we have explored in 'Chapter 4: Is it playful?', there are several elements of such a pedagogy that can be utilised in Key Stage 1 mathematics in order that the children's motivation and interest is maintained. Most notably these are that the playful process is highly valued, it offers opportunities for creative, flexible thinking and the testing of ideas, and it engenders high levels of engagement simply by being enjoyable. We have discussed how strategies for promoting playful mathematics can be incorporated in adult-led 'guided learning', and these can be replicated in Years 1 and 2 in order to scaffold children's growing understanding of place value and number facts, skills such as calculating and the effective use of resources to support problem-solving. Wherever possible, we can start with a problem, from any source, and play with it. The 'playful' approach we have outlined is transferable across all mathematics teaching, be that with individuals, small groups or whole classes, in any year group. It can be applied to the adaptation of any available lesson plans or schemes of work. We might call it by different names: 'exploration', 'investigation', 'enquiry'. . .; or recognise it in the mathematical thinking and behaviours we see our children exhibiting: 'curiosity', 'creativity', 'flexibility', 'reasoning', 'perseverance', 'engagement'...; but at heart, there is a need for us all to remain, and encourage others to be, joyfully and openly mathematically playful.

SUMMARY AND (SOME) CONCLUSIONS

In this chapter we have explored some of the opportunities and challenges present in mathematics for both teachers and children in the transition to Key Stage 1. We have highlighted where the EYFS and the Primary National Curriculum for mathematics provide us with overlapping purposes of and aims for the subject, and how continuing to develop strong foundations of playful interactions with purposeful mathematical problems, the use of multiple representations, talk and building connections is possible into Key Stage 1 and beyond.

Throughout each chapter, while acknowledging a need for children to develop a confident understanding of number, we have tried to emphasise that *pattern spotting* strongly connected with *spatial skills, measures, problem-solving* and *reasoning,* and *creativity* (particularly through developing a repertoire of ways to communicate mathematics) (Gifford, 2018) can also be identified as overarching goals towards which all mathematics teaching could build, and through which a deeper understanding of number and a wide knowledge of mathematics could develop. As Coles and Sinclair (2022) state, '...there's no such thing as best organisation...there are many possible routes to understanding mathematics which we need to keep exploring...It may be that students need what is seen as a more complex set of ideas, in order to make sense of the ideas considered to be the basics...Different aspects nurture each other and there is no obvious hierarchy in terms of what is most or least important' (p. 26).

We started this book with an exploration of different metaphors as a way of helping us to articulate our beliefs and perceptions about mathematics. If you consider those, or your own, again now, can you identify what each of them is saying about complexity? How are the different elements organised? Is there a sense of hierarchy? Are there start and finish points? How many? Where are the connections? How many are there? Where is the learner? Where are the risks? Where are the mistakes? Many of the discussions held around transition from Early Years/Reception into Year 1 and all the transitions in a child's school life that follow will focus on organisation and how this attempts to manage the complexity of human interaction with each other and mathematics.

Teaching is complex. Mathematics is complex. As you negotiate these complexities, it is worth remembering that your enthusiasm for and knowledge and beliefs about teaching *and* mathematics will have a greater impact on the experiences of the children in your care than any externally imposed curricula or assessments (Williams, 2008). Despite perennial efforts to standardise, mandate and control education, there can never be a simple, easily implemented curriculum or pedagogy that 'works'. Not completely. Not always. Not for everyone. As Biesta (2016) says,

> *...education always involves a risk. The risk is not that teachers might fail because they are not sufficiently qualified. The risk is not that education might fail because it is not sufficiently based on scientific evidence. The risk is not that students might fail because they are not working hard enough or are lacking motivation. The risk is there because, as W. B. Yeats has put it, education is not about filling a bucket but about lighting a fire. The risk is there because education is not an interaction between robots but an encounter between human beings. The risk is there because students are not to be seen as objects to be molded and disciplined, but as subjects of action and responsibility. Yes, we do educate because we want results and because we want our students to learn and achieve. But that does not mean that an educational technology, that is, a situation in which there is a perfect match between "input" and "output," is either possible or desirable. And the reason for this lies in the simple fact that if we take the risk out of education, there is a real chance that we take out education altogether.*
>
> (p. 1)

Mathematics education can be beautiful. It can be empowering. For everyone. Be brave.

> *...don't let yourself be sucked into an education that champions mathematics as pure logic, cold and heartless, a bunch of rules to follow. Who would want to learn that, or teach that? That is not where the heart of mathematics is. You cannot separate the proper practice of mathematics from what it means to be human...*
>
> *Believe that you and every person in your life can flourish in mathematics.*
>
> *This is an act of love.*
>
> (Su, 2020, p. 208)

FURTHER READING/RESOURCES

Bryce-Clegg, A. (2017). *Effective transition into Year 1*. Featherstone Education.

Clements, D., & Sarama, J. (2022). *Learning and teaching with learning trajectories*. https://www.learningtrajectories.org//learning-trajectories

Fisher, J. (2020). *Moving on to key stage 1: Improving transition into primary school.* Oxford University Press.

Morgan, D. (2022). *No need to differentiate in primary maths lessons.* https://www.ncetm.org.uk/features/no-need-to-differentiate-in-primary-school-maths-lessons/

Nrich. (2022). *Curriculum map.* https://docs.google.com/spreadsheets/d/1kYwPUMP-xu53c26sKywCk3tYYA74kgdrABIjAWnFyUfM/edit#gid=930038117

REFERENCES

Biesta, G. (2016). *The beautiful risk of education.* London: Routledge.

Boaler, J. (2022). *Mathematical mindsets: Unleashing students' potential.* Jossey-Bass.

Bryce-Clegg, A. (2017). *Effective transition into year 1.* Featherstone Education.

ClementsD., &SaramaJ. (2014). Learning trajectories: Foundations for effective, research-based education. In A.Maloney, J.Confrey, & K.Nguyen (Eds.), *Learning over time: Learning trajectories in mathematics education.* Information Age Publishing.

Clements, D., Sarama, J., Baroody, A. J., Joswick, C., & Wolfe, C. B. (2019). Evaluating the efficacy of a learning trajectory for early shape composition. *American Educational Research Journal, 56*(6), 2509–2531.

Coles, A., & Sinclair, N. (2022). *I can't do maths! Why children say it and how to make a difference.* Bloomsbury Education.

DfE. (2013). *The national curriculum in England Key stages 1 and 2 framework document.* https://assets.publishing.service.gov.uk/government/uploads/system/uploads/attachment_data/file/425601/PRIMARY_national_curriculum.pdf

DfE. (2021). *Statutory framework for the early years foundation stage.* https://assets.publishing.service.gov.uk/government/uploads/system/uploads/attachment_data/file/974907/EYFS_framework_-_March_2021.pdf

Drury, H. (2014). *Mastering mathematics: Teaching to transform achievement.* Oxford University Press.

Early Years Matters. (2022). *Transitions.* https://www.earlyyearsmatters.co.uk/eyfs/positive-relationships/transitions/

Fisher, J. (2020). *Moving on to key stage 1: Improving transition into primary school.* Oxford University Press.

Gifford, S. (2018). *New building blocks: A review of the pilot early learning goals.* NRICH.

Morgan, D. (2022). *No need to differentiate in primary maths lessons.* https://www.ncetm.org.uk/features/no-need-to-differentiate-in-primary-school-maths-lessons/

Ofsted. (2017). *Bold beginnings: The reception curriculum in a sample of good and outstanding primary schools.* https://assets.publishing.service.gov.uk/government/uploads/system/uploads/attachment_data/file/663560/28933_Ofsted_-_Early_Years_Curriculum_Report_-_Accessible.pdf

Sarama, J., & Clements, D. (2009). *Teaching math in the primary grades: The learning trajectories approach.* Young children, March, p. 63–64. National Association for the Education of Young Children.

Stripp, C. (2014). *Mastery in mathematics: What it is and why we should be doing it.* NCETM. https://www.ncetm.org.uk/features/mastery-in-mathematics-what-it-is-and-why-we-should-be-doing-it/

Su, F. (2020). *Mathematics for human flourishing.* Yale.

Williams, P. (2008). *Independent review of mathematics teaching in early years settings and primary schools.* Nottingham: DCSF.

INDEX